My Life, A Four-Letter Word

Confessions of a Counter Culture Diva

Dolores DeLuce

This book is dedicated to
Viva Marie Vinson, my daughter and the light of my
life.

INTRODUCTION

A VIEW
From Planet Couch

I am painfully aware of my lack in this strange new world past middle age where so-called Reality TV has made life cheaper than fast food and where any bimbo can gain fame and fortune for big hair, big mouths, big money, big tits, big families and no talent whatsoever. While Kathy Griffin was building her fortune by living *Life on the D List,* I was traveling even further down the scale, living my life on the XYZ list: X for X-RATED, Y for Y-BOTHER and Z for ZERO SELF ESTEEM.

I confess to spending long gaps of time wallowing in despair, with the flickering blue light and rays of radiation keeping me alive. Living on Planet Couch with the TV droning in the background didn't exactly breed success, and it's embarrassing to admit that if it weren't for the relationship I have with my grown daughter Viva today, television would be my only long-term companion.

I own no property, have no significant other and no grandchildren, and yet I defy the tyranny of nagging voices that tell me I didn't live my life right. Perhaps if I'd played by the rules, I might have been a credit to my parents and made it big in Hollywood. It was hard to see Johnny Carson retire in 1992 when I was forty-six, knowing I still had not fulfilled my showbiz fantasy—sitting on his set discussing my latest film or sitcom.

Modern technology has allowed me to never miss a moment of commercial-free TV viewing. With my trigger finger on the fast-forward button of my remote, I can watch an hour-long series in forty-five minutes, or a half-hour sitcom in twenty-two minutes, and feel good about all the time I'm not wasting. But there's a problem with any untreated addiction: it only gets worse. I can't imagine living without access to HBO and Showtime. Without television, what would I have to talk about?

I'm well aware that my mind, unguarded and poorly lit, is a fragile storage space, and if genes don't lie, I could end up like my mother—living out my twilight years with senile dementia in an Alzheimer's ward. The closer I draw to my final act, the more passionate I am to tell about the loves, lies, and lessons that will fill the dash between the dates of my birth and death that must one day appear on my tombstone.

When I turn off the TV long enough to look around my apartment, I notice the warm, peachy light that fills the space I've lived in for over thirty years. My spacious rent-controlled apartment, now an empty nest, is a stone's throw from the Pacific Ocean and the Venice Boardwalk. I smile at the photos in funky frames of me and my beautiful daughter in all the stages of our lives together. And adding to the clutter on every available shelf are the other pictures of my parents and siblings and their offspring, and my close friends, near and gone. I take great pleasure in the mementos that tell a story about who I am and where I've been.

In my bedroom, better known as the "shoe museum," I proudly display thirty pairs of high heels—or, as my friend Philipp likes to call them, "my mini-whore hooves." I was the Imelda Marcos of the welfare class. These shoes date from the Twenties to the Nineties and hang on three walls from an inch-thick molding a foot below my ceiling. The fourth wall features vintage platforms. My feet have grown tired of walking in them, but my eyes never tire of the hot pink, orange and fuchsia spikes, polka-dot and yellow-bowed pumps, and the gold-glitter tap shoes, all of which created the illusion I was more than five feet tall.

In my twenties, I was the size of an average fourth grader: four foot nine and three-quarter inches, and I could easily slip into a size-five shoe. Due to post-menopausal shrinkage, I'm now an even four foot eight, and can only wear a six wide flat. When I look up at my leopard spring-a-lators—the ones bought at Frederick's of Hollywood while shopping with Divine for the L.A. premiere of *Female Trouble*—I'm flooded with memories. The sight of platforms, the ones with the ornate cut-out Deco heels that my pretend husband Tommy dubbed my "Filipino jogging shoes," brings to mind the many nights he'd have to push me up the glistening, pre-dawn hills of San Francisco after dancing all night at the disco.

On the ledge are my Sixties black satin opera boots. In another spot rest my punk-rock, black-leather, spiked torture pumps—complete with bondage locks. My walls also feature two pair of sparkling rhinestone pointy-toed pumps I inherited from Tippy, the only petite drag queen I knew.

When I dust off the Forties open-toe pumps, I recall my performance as the Wacky WAC from Hackensack in the musical *Broken Dishes*. The star of my shoe collection is the pair of Carmen Miranda six-inch sparkling gold platforms. These show stoppers match the Golden Rays Vegas-style headdress I wore singing mock opera while portraying a sacrificial virgin to the Sun God, who changes her mind about being thrown into a volcano.

Despite all my praying to Saint Clare, the patron saint of television, I lost faith. When I turned thirty, I told myself that if I didn't make it in show business by forty, I'd gather up a sufficient stash of barbiturates and quietly check out. By the time I reached forty, I extended this pact even though I knew I could never do that to my daughter. By fifty, after surviving the grief-stricken years through the AIDS holocaust, I started to sum up my net worth by what my heart knows. And now I'm still here collecting Social Security and Medicare and thinking: Well, there's still Letterman!

This teenage girl trapped in a post-menopausal body is screaming to get out, so, *move over* sister hag, Kathy, who sold her memoir for two million; I have some priceless memories to write about too. After all, if Snooky from the *Jersey Shore* can write a book without having ever read one, my chances look pretty good. And even if my gems hold little interest to the world at large, for me they are precious pebbles collected at life's edge by the child still alive and kicking within me.

A FALL Preview

L ucille Ball is chanting in my brain. She won't shut up. She keeps asking, *"Who am I? Where am I? What am I?"*

"Shut up! I'm on stage at the Palace, a Chinese movie theatre in San Francisco, and Nixon is still in the White House."

Lucy says, *"Who's asking?"*

"I'm paranoid because I'm peaking. I shouldn't have dropped that acid."

Lucy keeps her interrogation up. *"What am I?"*

"I'm an orange Pumpkin with little green legs kicking wildly and the coachman and two dancing mice are pulling me from a cardboard pumpkin patch." Lucy is rolling her eyes at me.

"These are the facts and nothing but the facts ma'am." I tell Lucy like I'm the cop on *Dragnet*.

It's October 1973. A few minutes, or maybe a few hours ago, some stagehands squeezed me into this hollowed-out, orange day-glow beanbag that stretched over my green tights and leotard. I bobby-pinned a bright green curly wig to my head and glued gigantic glitter eyelashes over my eyes. They were flapping against my lids like sails in a windstorm. Then crayons were melting, splattering like rain in an MGM Musical all over my round pumpkin belly. When I put my hand on the beanbag, I remembered that it wasn't completely dry when they put it on me, and it still feels tacky.

The mice and coachman pry me loose and they're dragging me across the stage. When I look behind me, I notice I'm leaving a long, orange skid-mark on the stage floor. That can't be good. I close my eyes and through transparent lids I see a rainbow waterfall. When I open my eyes, I see it's a stream of lights spilling off pin spots attached to the beams on the ceiling. No matter how hard I close my lids, the lights keep pouring down like colored rain. The mice finally pull me to my feet, and a blinding white light hits me and now we're dancing to a Tchaikovsky overture. I remember all these steps. I did this dance a hundred times during rehearsals. But I didn't have the costume then.

Lucy makes a funny face and, just like Rickie, she says, *"You got some splainin' to do!"*

Yeah, the dress rehearsal, when everything was going haywire because half the costumes were unfinished; and Cinderella who is really Goldie Glitters, a six-foot-tall drag queen, was throwing a temper tantrum, and the director, who really is a choreographer, had a near-fatal heart attack. Or that's what I thought when I saw large veins popping from his neck as Goldie railed at him: "You have turned my dream into a nightmare." She was acting like one of those bitches in Chekhov's *Three Sisters*, the one who puts her hair up in the first act, takes it down in the second, and then pulls it out in the third.

Lucy started to laugh out loud.

Now it's all coming back to me. Pristine Condition, one of the ugly stepsisters, started the whole thing. Pristine—I call him Prissy—is my new best friend, and just a few

6

hours ago we were in my kitchen. Prissy is your average long-haired white boy, but he was in the middle of transforming himself into a Kewpie Doll when he gave me a hit of window-pane acid.

Just when the celluloid strip was melting on my tongue, Prissy went into a rant about growing up in Hereford, Texas. I thought he was exaggerating as he paced back and forth, telling me some Halloween horror story about when he found his mother dead with her head in the oven. Then Prissy got really agitated and started running and screaming to demonstrate how it was. And that's when he found his father in the den pulling the trigger of a shotgun jammed in his mouth. I laughed nervously and said, "Boy, girl, you have one hell of an imagination."

But Prissy got very quiet and, holding back tears, said, "I'm not making this shit up; that really happened, girl."

By the time we left the Castro, Prissy was in a better mood, but I was feeling guilty about leaving my three-year-old daughter with a sitter, even though I knew it was best. The show wouldn't start until midnight, way past her bedtime. I vaguely recall my driving down Geary Street to the Palace in North Beach, with blurry wavy lights and cars configured in paisley prints on the pavement. I was laughing so hard that tears fell from my eyes as Prissy ruthlessly dished Goldie. "You gotta take pity on the old girl. She's got varicose veins like the New York subway system. They run from the bottom of her feet clear up to her cock. That queen cast Prince Charming right off Castro after he let her blow him in the bathroom of "The Midnight Sun". Girl, you are the only new cast member who hasn't given anyone a blow job to get your part. Then Prissy told me that Prince Charming had a trick up under his crown for tonight's performance. "When Goldie drops her size-sixteen glass slipper, that swishy Prince is not going to run after her. He's planning to fit that slipper on his own foot.

Girl, just you wait and see. It'll be way funnier than that tired script those L.A. queers wrote."

When we drove past the Palace looking for parking, a mushroom cloud of marijuana smoke hovered over a sea of creatures of the night. Costumed freaks, transvestites, transients, and hookers were waiting for the Chinese patrons to vacate their movie theater. The smell of weed, chemicals, and incense followed us for several blocks to where I finally parked in a back alley. Prissy and I chanted *"nam myoho renge kyo"* to surround my VW Bug with white light that would hopefully deflect the police from noticing I parked in a red zone. As we walked toward the stage door, a streetcar dropped off a whole load of Judy Garland look-alikes, all singing, *"Clang, clang, clang, went the trolley. Ding, ding' goes the bell"*. They joined the crowd in front of the theatre as we slipped into the backstage door. When I finally got to a mirror, my makeup was a wreck, and the giant lashes were sticking to my cheeks.

With five minutes to Showtime, everyone was frantic. Suddenly, someone noticed that Prissy was missing, and I volunteered to help. She was outside, rolling in the gutter in her drag—a magnificent gold lamé couture gown made with inverted bra cups that accentuated the obvious: she was the flat-chested ugly step-sister. I picked up her wig, and with the help of two hot hunky guys, lured her back inside the theater. Prissy insisted on bringing through the stage door a gang of her fans for a free show.

By the end of my explaining, Lucy took a powder and I was back on stage.

Oh no, it's the finale and I'm still dancing. Here come the leaps. What was that director thinking? He knows I'm an untrained dancer.

Leap. Oh, this is a lot harder in a bean bag. Leap. Okay, just one more. Leap. What was I thinking when I dropped that acid? Okay, here goes nothing: the giant cartwheel finish.

Oops! I'm on the floor again and I can't get up. I'm flailing my little arms and legs. The audience is going wild; looks like my number is more hilarious than planned. I'm an overnight sensation.

As the mice help me up for our bows, I see the audience for the first time. I can see joints being passed down the rows and I hear liquor bottles rolling down the aisles and the applause feels like a tidal wave coming at me. The rowdy patrons are screaming catcalls as they hang off the balcony. The walls of the theatre are pulsating and the audience morphs into one big breathing organism of ecstasy and hedonism.

As I take my final bow, Divine is sitting in the front row, cheering me on and laughing her ass off. She looks like my long-lost alien mother as she winks with one of her overly exaggerated cat eyes.

Lucy pops up again, *"Who am I?"* She asks.

"I'm a star, just like Divine and all the others," I tell her.

My unscripted fall brought down the house, and in that moment I earned my place among the best of San Francisco's underground superstars. I wondered what took me so long to get here.

ACT I

IN THE BEGINNING WAS THE WORD

1

Pain

My name, Dolores, is taken from the Latin root word dolor, which means pain and sorrow. Underweight and incubated at birth, I caused her milk to dry up. That's how my mother, Gloria, a poor girl's Judy Holiday with a Jersey City accent, defended her choice not to nurse. "After the war when you was born, there was all that surplus rubber. They said the boob wasn't good for ya, that it wasn't hygienic. Artificial nipples was the rage."

In Latin cultures the name Dolores pays homage to the Mother of Sorrow, the Mother of Christ, Mary. However, when choosing my name, Gloria, the youngest of sixteen siblings wasn't thinking about the pain of the Virgin Mary—or the pain inherited from her Sicilian family. Gloria wasn't even thinking about the loss of her eighteen-inch waistline, or the labor it took to deliver me. There were just too many damn Mary's in our family, so Mom named me after Dolores Del Rio, her favorite movie star.

Dad added his own pain to the mix. John Grosso, the fourth child, born on the heels of a baby that died under mysterious circumstances, was named after his dead brother. After having four children in America, my grandparents took their young family back to Italy to reclaim the land they had left behind. Once back home in Serra, a lush village in the mountains east of Naples, they found no welcome. My grandfather had to fight a long, drawn-out court battle to win the rights of his property back from his cousin who had been caretaking the land. By the time my grandma was pregnant with the last of their eight children, Grandpa finally won back his property. On the walk home from the courthouse, Granddad's embittered cousin shot him. My father was only ten when he saw his father shot to death. My grandmother managed to send each of her US-born children back to the States, one by one, to hold claim to their American citizenship. At seventeen, my father buried his pain on the bloodstained land and returned to join his older siblings in New York.

***

My earliest memories are of overcast New Jersey skies. My skinny Uncle Ernie is back from the war and sleeping on a cot in the living room; I'm running to Mom, crying because the boy next door peed on me. The only other image I still hold of our post-WWII flat in Elizabeth is a long flight of steps that led up to our second-floor apartment where three vivid events happened. I recall Mom carrying a bundle up the steps and Daddy following behind her with a suitcase. I remember my aunt making a big fuss and telling me the bundle's name was Ginny, short for Virginia, another name for the Virgin Mary. When I was two I recall seeing sad Grandma for the first time as she labored slowly up the steps. She was dressed all in black, and my father was thin and handsome, walking behind her carrying her luggage.

And then there was the day in 1949 that changed my life forever, the day Dad brought home the television set.

I was three years old and I had no idea what to expect. With my face wedged between the railings on the landing, I watched while Dad and Uncle Ernie struggled to get the gigantic cardboard box up each step. Once the box was in the living room, Dad cut through the cardboard with a bread knife and revealed a large wooden box with a round glass hole in the middle.

We were the first family in our neighborhood to have a television, and there was much excitement as our relatives and neighbors crowded into the small apartment for the Zenith's arrival.

Delicious smells of sausage and peppers mixed with my uncles' cigars wafting through the atmosphere thick with laughter. Mom even took off her apron with the cherries on it and left the sauce cooking on the stove to show off her new polka dotted dress. Dad and Uncle Ernie lifted up the television as if it was the Madonna statue I saw in a procession at the Feast of San Gennaro, and held it with reverence as Dad contemplated the best place to put it.

I sat patiently on Mom's new flowered couch covers with my legs dangling and watched Dad staple the long antenna wires to the wall so the rabbit ears would work. My Aunt Anna made a late entrance in her fancy new mink. The ladies made a fuss over her, but my mother huffed and walked away. Finally, Dad plugged in the television, and all the grownups turned away from Aunt Anna's coat to look back at the TV. Mom smiled and Aunt Anna excused herself to the powder room.

I moved closer and sat cross-legged on the floor just inches from the glass screen. I was pretending to be a little gnome because I was sitting in a forest of grownups' legs. Dad turned on the switch and a pop of light came up, and in the middle of the glass were grey, black, and white circles. It's a good thing that sausage and meatballs were waiting in the kitchen because the grownups got bored fast looking at the test pattern, and when Mom yelled, "Dinner's ready," all the tree trunks scurried off. I stared at the test pattern for a very long time, waiting for something wonderful to happen. Nothing did, but I had faith that if I kept watching, it would.

By the end of that year, Dad had managed to save enough money from peddling with his mobile fruit and vegetable bus to put a down payment on a two-story home in Paterson, New Jersey. So he packed our precious TV and all our furniture, wrapped me in a blanket, and put me next to the dishes inside an orange crate. Then he slid me under the produce shelves of his peddling bus during the long ride to our new house.

From the orange crate, I could see my mom sitting up front on one of the kitchen chairs, holding onto the driver's seat with one hand and the bundle called Ginny with the other. The glassware did not complain, but I cried loudly in order to be heard over the engine and the grinding, shifting gears of the rattling old bus. Finally, Dad pulled over on the highway and came toward the bin where I was stashed. He bent down close to me and yelled, "Stop you're cryin' before I give you something to cry about." Learning not to cry was a tall order for a girl with my name and nature.

2

Loud

I preferred my black-and-white companions that lived in the TV over the outdoor view of bleak New Jersey skies, which clouded most of my childhood. I especially preferred TV drama to the high-decibel scenes played out around our family table.

On spaghetti night in a kitchen that always smelled of tomato sauce, garlic, parmesan, linoleum wax, and Ajax, Mom passed a big bowl of pasta from Grandma to Dad.

"John, that S.O.B. gave your cousin Millie a cheap, used fur. It was damaged goods, just like her, and now she thinks he's gonna marry her."

"Gloria, can you pass me the *brasiolli*?" Dad asked.

"And your sister, she's another one, that *cappo fresca*. She told Ma that I waste your hard-earned money on too much food. She's got a lot of nerve," Mom said.

"For Christ's sake, Gloria, my mother can hear you," Dad said.

"Since when does ya mother talk English?"

Ginny, my little sister with a springy curl in the middle of her forehead, pipes up in her singsong voice, "Mommy, mommy, look."She holds out her empty bowl. "I cleaned my plate just like you told me. Can I have some more?"

Mom scooped out another portion from the bowl. "Of course, sweetheart, you're such a good eater. I wish your sister Dee would eat like you."

At that point I stood on the leatherette kitchen chair and, like the grownups I'd seen at my cousin Loretta's wedding, I clinked my glass to get attention. Clink, clink, clink — "Hey everybody, everybody" — clink, clink. "Shut up," I was yelling now. "I've got something important to say." All moving mouths came to a standstill. "When I grow up, I'm going to Hollywood and I'm gonna be an actress." In just five short years, my Mom had convinced me that Dad was someone to fear if I stepped out of line. But my father had never raised a hand to me, and although I was sitting across the table out of his reach, I could feel the sting of his slap.

"Over my dead body!" Dad yelled. "No daughter of mine will ever be an actress. They're all *'puttana'*."

I was only five, but somehow I knew that was Italian slang for 'whore'. From that day on I secretly practiced acting and used it to convince Mom that I was sick enough to stay home from school while she went off to work at the factory. I was a good little method actress. I could actually give myself a fever.

Lying in my parent's bed and pretending to be sick, I would watch Mom get ready for work. I loved her vanity table with the beautiful beveled mirror glass and gold-trimmed tray where she kept her matching comb and hairbrush. After putting the last of the bobby pins in place to keep her wavy hair off her face, she would open the gold lipstick tube and twist it until the tube came all the way up to the top. I studied her technique. First, she'd run the deep red over her bottom lip, then carefully outline the two points of her top lip before she mashed her lips together to spread the creamy red evenly. Then she'd pluck a tissue from the matching gold Kleenex holder, place it between her lips, and blot. After one last glance in the mirror, Mom would come over to the bed and kiss me on the cheek, leaving an imprint of cherry lips.

Sometimes when she wasn't in a rush, Mom would share nuggets of truth about her childhood, like how she dropped out of eighth grade when her dad died and went to work to help her sick mother. She admitted she didn't like school, so it wasn't such a sacrifice. These were always my favorite times with my mother, when I had her to myself. I felt sad that she was leaving, yet the minute I heard her latch the door lock behind her a flood of freedom engulfed me. With everyone gone, only my grandmother was left to watch me.

For the most part, Grandma lived within the confines of her mind and her room in the attic, so I had free run of the house. In all her years in America, Grandma learned only a few words of English, her favorite being 'shit', which she pronounced, *Shee-ta;* the other was the name of the downtown department store, Quankenbush. "*Io va a la Quaken-a-bush-a,*" she said every time she went downtown to buy her favorite cotton panties or a new black dress.

She'd come out of her room just long enough to throw some leftover cold spaghetti in a pan with a half-cup of olive oil and serve me lunch on a tray in front of the TV. With Grandma, I could do no wrong except for this one day when she caught me belting out a popular song, the number one hit on the *Hit Parade, 'Hoopdi Do'.* My family and I watched the Hit Parade religiously on Saturday nights. There I was, spinning in circles and howling at the top of my lungs, "*Hoopdi, do, Hoopdi do, I get a fever when I think about you, Hoopdi- do, Hoopdi- do.*"

At first I didn't hear Grandma hollering, half in Italian, half broken English, "*Stata chi, stata-chi, shut up-a-you-*

mouth, bad-a-word." Then she screamed even louder, "*A fon cool-a-di-sodada!*" and marched back to her room, slamming the door behind her. I couldn't figure out why she was so mad. Later that evening Mom scolded me. "You owe Grandma an apology. I know she can be a pain but you know better than to curse at your grandmother."

"Ma, I didn't curse. I was just singing '*Hoopdi do, hoopdi do.*'" Mom rolled her eyes, then laughed. Oh, I guess she heard it wrong; she said you were singing, '*Foot-i do, foot-i do.*"

"What's that mean?"

"Don't ever sing it around her again. It means 'up yours'."

"Mom does, *a fon-cool-a-di-sodada,* mean, 'do you want ice with your soda?'"

Mom suddenly had one of her laughing fits that caused her to wet her pants. As she rushed off to the toilet, she said, "I'll tell you when you get older."

***

During the weeks that the *Million Dollar Movie* showed my favorite films—the musicals and romantic comedies of the '30s and '40s—I managed to extend one sick day into a week. *The Million Dollar Movie* repeated the same film five times a day, for a full week. I learned every line to every song ever written for those films. If it had been that easy to learn the multiplication tables, I might not need a calculator now to multiply anything over five times ten.

I imagined that I was an alien from another planet who had been left on Earth with this family. Anyone not on TV was an obstacle to the world I would live in one day. If Lou Costello could make it from Paterson to Hollywood, then so could I. Hadn't I been named after a movie star? Even on bright sunny days I preferred watching TV to playing outside with my sister and pesky cousins, who kept emigrating from Italy every few years to take up residency in our basement. In my TV haze I couldn't tell one cousin from another, especially since they were all named Frank or Mary—with the exception of the ones who had Italian first names I couldn't pronounce.

I took solace from my companions who lived inside the box; dancing with Fred and Ginger in *Carefree* or skating with Sonja Henie in *the Countess of Monte Cristo*. I dreamed I'd fall in love one day like Ava Gardner with Jimmy Walker in *One Touch of Venus*, or magically grow up really fast like Jennifer Jones did in *A Portrait of Jenny*, so she could catch up and be with her true love, the much older Joseph Cotton.

After watching *The Countess of Monte Cristo* twenty-one times, I wanted to be an Olympic champion figure skater like its star, Sonja Henie. Sonja, with her sidekick posing as her maid, ends up at a fancy ski lodge where she enters a skating contest as the Countess of Monte Cristo. After checking in, the girls realized they had nothing fancy to wear, so the Countess tears down the elaborate hotel draperies and whips up two evening dresses and a cute skating outfit for the competition. This movie ignited my passion for sewing and ice skating.

Months before Christmas that year, I started bugging my folks for ice skates. With Dad up and out at 5 a.m. six days a week and Mom at the factory all day there was little time to take me to the ice rink for lessons, but they broke down and bought me my first pair of skates. By mid-January I tired of standing with the rubber guards over the blades on the worn-out Persian carpet, so I tried to skate on Mom's shiny, waxy kitchen linoleum. Mom took pride in her floor. "It's so clean you could eat off it." That night when she got home from the factory and saw the damage I had done, Mom grabbed the broom and chased me around the house.

"You little bastard, I'll kill you! Just wait until your father gets home!"

I kept running in circles and she kept missing me. I ran clear down the steps and into the basement, but she finally caught up to me. "I've had it with you and that friggin' TV givin' you ideas. *Basta!*" She came down hard on my head with the broom. "Here's your Academy Award, you dumb Dago bitch!"

It only encouraged me.

Although I hated the bitter damp of Jersey winters, I bundled up and went outside in below-freezing temperatures. Mom took away my TV for two whole weeks, so I decided to create my own practice rink. Somewhere I learned that if you used hot water, it would freeze faster than cold, so I lugged bucket after bucket of hot water from the basement sink to use for my project. There in a 5'x5' corner between our neighbor's fence and the side of our two-story house, I poured the first bucket of scalding hot water, and by the time I returned with the next bucket, that layer would be solid and I'd pour another. This went on for several more trips to the basement until I made an ice patch large enough to practice figure eights.

Alone on that thin slick of ice I skated in circles until dark, dreaming of the day when I could skate away.

Mom and Dad

The Grosso Family, 1951

Me & Ginny, Flower Girls at Cousin Loretta's Wedding

Grandma Grosso in front of Dad's peddling bus

3

Diet

By the time I was twelve, my vocabulary had expanded along with my waistline. Chub, Fats, Lies, and Love underscored the excess-fat breakout on my upper arms, boobs, thighs, and tummy. My sister Ginny, the good eater, had been the chubby one until I got my first period. Before that catastrophe, I could squeeze into Mom's wedding dress with the eighteen-inch waistline and button up every satin button. Mom no longer dreamed of getting back her girlish figure, and it appeared to me that only the men in our family stayed slim. When the women hit thirty, it was time to shop at Lane Bryant's. The females on my father's side suffered from the Grosso family curse. The word 'grosso' means big in Italian, and since most of the gals never grew taller than five feet, all that cannoli had to go somewhere.

When the whole clan gathered for what they called their 'cousins' club'—basically a monthly excuse to gorge—the feed was on with an eight-course dinner from antipasto to desserts. After everyone inhaled a pasta course, which included meatballs, sausage, pork, and beef from the gravy, then the main meat dish followed, which was either a roast or chicken with roasted potatoes, vegetables, and salad on the side. As soon as they cleared the dishes, out came the coffee, and the women carried trays of homemade desserts to the table. I watched as each lady sampled every one of a dozen assorted Italian pastries. "I never eat like this at home; I don't understand why I can't lose any weight." This was the mantra they all shared.

I was determined to shake the Grosso curse. Again, television provided the answer. I found a solution through the wonders of TV workouts with Jack La Lane and the popular diet shake, Metrical—the Slim Fast of the '50s. I was convinced this combo was a sure-fire way to get me in shape for stardom. My urgency to get to Hollywood had only heightened with puberty and the discovery of my first true love, who rode through my TV on a *Wagon Train*. At first sight of Robert Horton, a tall, handsome, redheaded cowboy, I knew he was for me. Unlike my previous crushes, boys like Donny of the Mousekateers, or Marty of the *Mickey Mouse Club* spin-off series, *Spin and Marty*, Robert was a real man. There was something about the way he wore his guns down low around his hips that got my juices flowing.

With the aid of vinegar rinses on my hair before going out in the sun, I commenced a natural beauty routine that I was convinced would change my brunette hair to a sandy blond like Gidget's. I spent that whole summer smelling like vinegar whenever I broke a sweat. Along with this cockamamie beauty tip, I thought all I had to do was increase my workouts with Jack LaLane and replace my meals with Metrical.

The only way I could swallow the chalky chocolate-like substance without gagging was to fantasize that I was on the set of *Wagon Train* with Robert Horton in his trailer, and we were sharing a Metrical Cocktail. I'd take a sip and say, "Oh my darling, you are such an inspiration. If it weren't for you, I could never get through my sit-ups today." Robert would lick his lips and move closer. He'd place his big man hands around my tiny waist and I could feel his six shooters press against my body as he breathed in my ear, "You're almost down to eighteen inches, baby. Keep this up and I'll get you a small part on the show."

Nothing short of an atom bomb would keep me from watching my cowboy lover every Wednesday at 8 p.m. Eastern Standard Time. So you can imagine my predicament when Mom decided to schedule her first piano lesson for that exact hour. Our piano was located in the dining room next to our adjoining living room, just inches away from the TV. So while the folks were digesting dinner in the backyard, and with less than an hour before show time, I took it upon myself to redecorate. I figured I could move the large console TV into my bedroom, at least temporarily. Then I could shut the door and have an uninterrupted hour of romance.

I had less than twenty minutes to drag the heavy mahogany set over carpets and hardwood. The TV was as big horizontally as our refrigerator was vertical. I single-handedly moved it through half the house while removing several yards of antenna wiring that was stapled all along the baseboard of the living room. How I managed this feat I'll never know, but with all the strength of a frantic mother saving the life of her child crushed under the wheel of a car, I moved that console unit all the way from the living room, through the dining room, and into my bedroom.

When my folks came upstairs with the piano teacher, and Dad noticed the furniture rearrangement, he came at me full-force. As the piano teacher cowered in a corner, Mom tried to hold him back. "John, stop it already, what will people think?" In his frustration Dad picked up my very first pair of high-heeled pumps, red patent-leather, two-inch chubby heels that Mom bought me the same day we went shopping for my training bra. One shiny shoe flew overhead like a B-52 Mustang bomber and hit the crucifix on the wall, knocking Jesus to the floor. The matching pump followed, hitting me smack in the middle of my forehead as Dad kept ranting, "And no more high heels and lipstick!"

Wagon Train went off the air and I took a hiatus from dieting. Without Robert in my life, I resorted to mixing Metrical with chocolate ice cream

4

Boys

I was only nine when I got my first period, and I went from Daddy's little girl to Daddy's big problem. Along with becoming a woman at age nine came the horrible cramps. I was still so little, and my dad couldn't bear to see me in so much pain. To help me relax, he would pour me a double shot of sweet vermouth and then gently tickle my arms until I fell asleep.

Between grades six and eight, I had gone from a training bra to a C-cup, and Alan Din took notice. Alan was taller and cuter than any of the six boys in my eighth-grade class, and he was my first crush who wasn't a TV star. Alan Din was also the only non-white boy at St. Anthony's, and the first person I ever knew from a racially mixed marriage. I learned the meaning of Eurasian after seeing Jennifer Jones in *Love Is A Many Splendored Thing*. Alan's mother was a white British woman and his father was Chinese. After school, Alan and I would walk hand-in-hand while he carried my books. On the stoop leading to the porch, Alan gave me my first kiss, a peck on the lips. Over dinner that evening, I realized that Grandma witnessed the event from her attic window and had told my dad, "If Dee ever marries that Chink, at least I could get my shirts done for free."

In Paterson, the only Chinese people we ever saw were the ones who owned and operated Chinese laundries or restaurants, which we frequented often since Mom's favorite thing to do besides cooking was "to go out for Chinks." As my mom laughed at Dad's rude joke, I sat solemnly like Jennifer Jones, knowing my romance was doomed. I should have known that my father would have no tolerance for any boy unless he was all-white, Catholic, and Italian.

In my family, sex lectures started early. Over coffee percolating, I listened to my mother's stories about poor girls in Italy who would sooner drown themselves in a well than bring disgrace upon their families. Like Maxwell House Coffee, my mom was chock-full of contradictions: one minute expounding on the virtue of virginity, and the next gossiping about her in-laws, or telling gleeful tales about disreputable women.

Mom would also often allude to a dirty secret about my grandma that was best left at the bottom of the pot with the stale coffee grounds. According to her, if Grandma had abided by the rules that seem to apply only to girls, none of us would be here today—two generations of Italian Americans flushed down a well.

According to Mom, when Grandma was sixteen she got knocked up by Grandpa while he was engaged to her older sister. To save the family from disgrace, a double shotgun wedding was quickly arranged. Grandpa married Grandma and her older sister was pawned off on Grandpa's older brother. Then both newlywed couples were shipped off to America before any evidence of my grandma's sin appeared. How my mother learned this story, or if it was even true, I'll never know.

By high school I started looking at boys whose last names ended in vowels. Auggie Matterazzo or Auggie-Doggy or Auggie Mattress, as the kids called him, was tall for a fourteen-year-old freshman and had the added advantage of being a great dancer. With him, I won all the CYO (Catholic Youth Organization) dance contests. Auggie could do a mean *mashed potatoes* but he would always complain of a back ache when he had to bend over to reach me for a slow dance. For our first Christmas together I hand-knitted Auggie the first complete sweater I ever made. On New Year's Eve I asked him why he never wore the crew neck pullover.

"My mother left it under the tree and the dog ate it." With that Auggie/Doggy got his walking papers.

Not long after, I took up with another gangster in training named Dominic Avitabale. Dom and I had perfect chemistry and he was the right height for slow dancing. On one occasion in the church basement while Mass was in session we almost went all the way. Dom was at second base when from overhead we heard the Choir's singing *'Kyrie-e-lei-son'*. He stopped abruptly.

"What's wrong?" I asked.

"It's bad enough we're missing Mass, but if we go all the way, you know what will happen to us!" he said.

"They're both mortal sins, we might as well get some fun out of it if we're going to burn in Hell for all eternity," I said.

Although Dom was into gambling and even ate meat on Fridays, he had been a good altar boy and he believed it was in his own best interest to preserve the prize for our wedding night. He quickly zipped up his fly and tucked his white button-down-collar shirt into his pants and led me back upstairs to catch the end of mass.

Even my dad accepted Dom as his future son-in-law. It gave Dad a good argument for not paying for college.

"It's a waste of money for a girl," Dad said. "Once you get married your husband will support you." Where he got that idea, I don't know, since my mother was still waiting tables after eighteen years of marriage.

After three and a half years of dates at the bowling alley ending with heavy make-out sessions in the bucket seats of his 1963 hard-top convertible Thunderbird, I began to get restless. Slowly I began to realize the limitations of a future with Dom. According to the Church and my parents, any choice other than the nunnery or marriage to Dom and living in an aluminum-sided two-story house within walking distance from my parents' was the wrong one. But I broke up with him anyway. I just wanted something more than a small-town boy could offer.

Saints & Sinners

Volume #2 — Edition #1 — Blessed Sacrament Church — C.Y.O. & Dismas Club Price 15¢ — January 1963

COUPLE OF THE MONTH

By Celia Swin

This month our spotlight is on a couple, not too big in size, but who make up for it in their personalities. They've been going together for one year and six months. You can find them riding around in a Thunderbird.

ABOUT THE BOY: He was born July 28, 1944 and is a graduate of Eastside. He is now attending Fairleigh Dickenson and studying law. He loves bowling, dancing, golfing, chicken, steak, and of course — his girl. PS. He hates vegetables!

ABOUT THE GIRL: She was born ...

of the Lord." You recall I'm sure, the various events surrounding the birth of Our Saviour. There was the response of the shepherds and then the response of Herod to the announcement of Christ's birth. To the shepherds this was a gloriously joyous experience. Their souls soared aloft in hope and peace and joy. To Herod the announcement represented a threat, it disturbed him, caused him to become an evil, suspicious, even murderous person.

The birth of Christ for us is primarily a spiritual experience, something happens inside us. Either we resemble the the shepherds and ...

Dee and Dom at the Prom, 1963

5

Jobs

My parents had strong work ethics and when I turned fourteen they insisted I give up freeloading and my lucrative allowance of fifty cents a week and get a part-time, minimum-wage job.

The Children and Young Persons Act had set fourteen as the minimum age at which children could work, and the minimum wage was $1.15 an hour.

At my first job I assembled catalogues and brochures for mail-order packets that were remotely related to fashion at a collating factory. Every Saturday morning I stood in front of a long row of twenty small wooden slates that resembled a conveyor belt. This conveyor belt was unlike the ones I had seen on *I Love Lucy* when Lucy and Ethel worked at the candy factory. The belt stood still while I did all the work.

That summer I was hired as a dishwasher/bus girl at Boscarino's Italian Bistro, a charming ma-and-pa neighborhood eatery. When it got busy, I got to help Ma Boscarino carry food out to the customers and bus tables. It was a relief to leave the kitchen, where I was stuck at the sink. It wouldn't have been so bad except that whenever I was up to my elbows in dirty, greasy tomato dish water, my boss, old Pa Boscarino, would leave the pasta boiling and come up from behind, put his slimy paws on my boobs, and push his hard-on against my ass. I probably would have endured this abuse and held onto the job if it hadn't been for the swinging door between the kitchen and dining room. It swung in both directions and the glass window was too high for me to see if anyone was coming in from the other side. On a day when I was carrying a tray of food out to the dining room, I accidently pushed the swinging door open into Ma Boscarino while she was carrying a tray of dirty dishes back into the kitchen. Glass and pasta flew all over the joint. I assume Ma had an inkling that Pa had been trying to stuff his noodle up my behind because, she fired me the minute I finished cleaning up all the mess. With employment opportunities like this, I was learning that the dirtiest of all the four-letter words was 'work'.

After the Ma and Pa spaghetti fiasco, I learned to press men's dress shirts and pants at a neighborhood dry cleaner where I was fired because I couldn't keep the seams straight on the men's trousers. I also inspected winter coats for threads and loose buttons at a small factory owned by my sister's boyfriend's grandparents.

I also worked at the same Woolworth's where my mother worked as a snack bar waitress. Luckily, I was placed way at the very back of the store in hardware, where no one I knew from school would see me. I got so bored that I'd punch holes in the plastic-packaged tools just to alleviate my anxiety. I found a way to increase my minimum wage when I realized that if a customer gave me the exact amount for their purchase, I could avoid ringing up the sale and pocket the cash. I got so brazen that I often pushed the customers to come up with the exact change.

Over the span of my junior and senior high school years, I had had more bad jobs than runs in my stockings.

For my next experiment in low-class living, I tried my hand at meat wrapping.

At a small neighborhood market in Clifton, New Jersey, I shared the market basement with my co-meat wrapper Gloria Zappo, a high school dropout who was dumber than mice, and two of the most horrible specimens of the male sex in New Jersey. These two butchers—Neil, a lanky, sandy thin-haired, hen-pecked married man, and Dick, a short, fat greaseball—were the X-rated version of Abbot and Costello. Once Gloria and I wrapped the steaks, roasts, and poultry in plastic, we would take turns carrying them upstairs to fill the meat cases. Back in the 1960s, most of the customers were female. If the customer needed a special cut of meat, she would have to call down on the intercom system and ask the butcher. Each day we heard, "Oh butcher, oh butcher, can you trim the fat off this T-bone for me," or, "Butcher, butcher can you please grind this piece of sirloin?"

To which Neal would reply, after switching off the intercom and grabbing his crotch, "Grind this!"

And then Dick would touch himself and chime in, "I got your tube steak right here." It was a doo-wop medley of *trim this* and *grind that,* all the day long. It was bad enough that these two pervs sexually harassed me and Gloria, but what they did to the poor lady customers was even worse. Dick, the more grotesque of the two, would send me up to fetch the special piece of meat and then, once I brought it back downstairs, he'd put it into the grinder—but before he'd hand it back to me for re-sealing, he spit into it. It took me many years before I could enjoy a burger or a meatball again.

After six months of that bloody hell, my dad used his position as produce manager at the Shoprite to get me a coveted union job in the illustrious meat-wrapping industry.

The only complaint I had with Shoprite besides working so close to my dad was the unflattering butcher's smock and hairnet I had to wear, and the mustached middle-aged co-wrappers who worked beside me. On days when I accidentally on purpose forgot my hair net, Mary, the one with the thickest mustache and telltale beard, would always loan me her spare. Whenever the tedium got the best of me, I'd dress up a chicken in my hairnet and talk to it to amuse myself and annoy my co-workers.

6

Lust

My male cousins had free rein to sow their wild oats, but when it came to the girls, fuggedaboutit'! If my parents wanted to keep me a virgin, they should have named me Virginia, the other name for Mary, the virgin, like my good sister.

The summer after high school graduation, while working at the Shoprite, I met Johnnie, the box boy, a dead ringer for Frankie Avalon. Johnnie took pride in his slicked-back pompadour and was a man of few words. He had only one obvious flaw: he was married. The wedding to his high school sweetheart happened so fast after graduation that her bridesmaids wore their prom dresses.

Behind my father's back, right there in the stock room, hidden between the rows of crated canned peaches and boxes of baked macaroni and cheese, I let Johnnie get to second base. I said *yes* to his advances, knowing all too well that a married man, like all men, as my mother told me, "wanted one thing only." I was hell-bent on giving it to him. Despite Mom's warnings about men who won't buy the cow if you give the milk for free, or her other classic, "If you let him buy you a hot dog, he'll try to squeeze it out of you," I had no resistance to a free hot dog.

Johnnie breathed heavily into my ear and whispered, "Hey babe, how about I swing by your place later and take ya for a burger." A meat wrapper unwrapped by a box boy was my inevitable destiny. It was so *These Are the Days of Our Lives* in New Jersey.

Sitting on the curb outside my house, I wondered about what it would feel like when my cherry popped. When Johnnie pulled up and I jumped in to his '63 Ford Fairlane convertible, he barely came to a full stop. He laid rubber as he peeled off and told me there was no time for a stop at the White Castle. He had just gotten word that his wife had gone into early labor. Yeah, right, about five months early, but that didn't stop Johnnie from keeping his date with me. Without even as much as a cherry coke, he drove directly to the parking spot and got right to it. After all of my mother's bloody stories about first-time sex, I wasn't expecting a good time, but what followed was a shock. After less than five minutes of heavy petting, he put his penis in me. With no pain, no blood, no feeling whatsoever, and after just three thrusts, he ejaculated and it was over. I was so startled by the brevity of the act and lack of drama that I laughed out loud.

"Is that it?" I was still dazed and confused when Johnnie dropped me at the curb outside my house moments later, but I was grateful the deed was done.

7

Date Rape

For the next chapter of my young adult life, I learned the theme song "I'm Jist a Girl Who Cain't Say No" from the film version of *Oklahoma.*

For my eighteenth birthday, Dom's sister, Angela, took me to see my first Off-Broadway musical, *The Fantasticks.* The character El Guyio, a handsome, seductive gypsy, was played by a young Jerry Orbach. In the play, El Guyio is hired by the parents of a young couple to stage a mock rape in order to dissuade the ingénue from going too far out into the real world. It's all done to music and makes rape look like a walk in the park. It wasn't the first lie the wonderful world of entertainment ever told me.

My friend Lucille's parents were Italian immigrants who were far stricter than mine, and wouldn't let her date even after graduation. Because I felt sorry for her, I let her use me as a cover to get out of the house. Lu would show up at my house early to rat her hair and apply pink lipstick and heavy black eyeliner and slip into a tight mini. On one too many occasions I had let Lucille talk me into going with her on blind dates. Growing more brazen in her pursuit of freedom, Lu planned for us to travel up to West Point where we were to meet up with her new boyfriend and his buddy, both military men, who had promised a picnic lunch and tour of The Point.

We told my folks that we were taking a drive upstate to see the leaves turn colors. I drove my first car, a yellow 1959 Fiat Convertible that I bought with my meat-wrapping money. My cousin Frankie warned me that Fiats were not reliable, and said that F.I.A.T. stood for Fix It Again, Tony, but I didn't care because my car looked as cool as an XKE Jaguar. Because I'm so short, I couldn't drive it until my dad rigged the clutch and brake pedals with wooden blocks so that my feet could reach the floor. Within a week I burnt out the clutch. But none of that mattered now, I was on the highway headed north with the wind in my hair, and I felt free—until we reached our destination and I met my blind date.

How Lucille found these characters, I'll never know, but I will never forget that afternoon. As I got into the back seat of her boyfriend's car, my date—blond, tall, red-faced and red-necked—shimmied over to my side of the car, put his arm around me, and in the most charming southern accent said, "Hi, my name is Big Bob and I'm from Mississippi, where we drown niggers in the river." It was 1963 and he wanted this little northern girl to know where he stood on the Civil Rights issue. I kept my mouth shut and refrained from mentioning that my favorite folk song was, *"We Shall Overcome."*

As Lu's date drove us around the Point giving us a tour, I realized that these two good old boys were not officers or gentlemen as I had imagined they would be. They were enlisted men with deep-seated resentments against the privileged officers in training at the Academy. Lu's date bragged about how they had free reign of the entire base, since they were in fact the Military Police.

Our host drove off the road into a thick wood that was well hidden from the main road. The car came to a stop and out we piled. The boys marched around to the trunk to get the picnic lunch they had promised and came back with several six-packs of beer. It wasn't long before Lucille disappeared with her beau behind a colorful bush and left me alone with the boozy booby prize.

I drank a whole beer on an empty stomach and without any further conversation, Big Bob started to make out with me. Now, if I was on my turf in the city and he wasn't packing a weapon, I might have said something like, "Excuse me but I don't make out with bigots." There was no ladies' room to run off to powder my nose, and I couldn't think of another excuse or escape.

Within moments we were on a large flat rock and Big Bob had pulled down my panties and then his own skivvies to reveal his business. Big Bob had earned his name. Oh my god, the thing was scary. Granted, I had only seen two other penises, but this appendage held little resemblance to those. Big Bob was a freak show. I didn't have a ruler on me, but I'd say it was no less than a foot long and very, very fat. Big Bob did his best to get some of it inside of me and all I felt was pain. Luckily it was over as fast as it all began and when he got off of me, I noticed the blood I had been promised. I could clearly see that what Johnnie had not accomplished, Big Bob had. There it was, the skin of my hymen, stuck to my thigh and mixed with the fallen leaves on the flat rock beneath me.

I don't recall what happened after that, but somehow I was back on the road popping the clutch and grinding the gears of my Fiat. That was the last time I would ever let Lucille take advantage of my easy-going nature.

8

Free Bird

Out from under my father's roof, I lay on the earth with only a sleeping bag beneath me and the stars above, sipping a taste of freedom. It was 1965, and I was at the Newport Folk Festival in Rhode Island. With the music and lyrics of Judy Collins, Richie Havens, Joan Baez and Bob Dylan swirling in my brain, I caught a vision of a life beyond New Jersey. There was promise of revolution in the air and I sucked up each breath the way I had when I was a kid pretending to smoke candy cigarettes. I inhaled dreams deeply into my lungs, and exhaled a decision to leave home for good.

That same summer I got to see Dylan two more times, first at Forest Hills Country Club, and then at Madison Square Garden, and by that fall I was almost ready to break away from my family. Since I had graduated high school, the highlight of my social life had been going to Greenwich Village. At least there I could bump up against others like myself, but I would always have to end the night by heading back home via the bridge or tunnel. I went back to the Italian Provincial furniture of my twin-bed set in the room that I still shared with my sister, and back to the boring day job in a cold meat locker where I still worked under the nose of my father. If working in a freezer and wearing a hair net wasn't a strong enough motivator for change, I had an even more urgent reason to leave. Dating danger and living a lie, I knew if my father ever caught me doing what I did behind his back, he might kill me.

Once I would no longer allow my friend Lucille to use me as her cover, she took her revenge by telling my sister's best friend about me and a black boy I had dated a few times in the Village. The day I found out Ginny knew about him, I was sitting in bed on my messy side of our room, reading *Go Tell It on the Mountain,* by James Baldwin, while Ginny tidied up her neat side of our room. Joan Baez was on the stereo and Ginny was singing along to "Black is the Color of My True Love's Hair," one of my favorite tracks. Ginny inched over to my side as she sang even louder and stood at the edge of my bed. Suddenly she snatched my book out of my hands and we were eye to eye as she sang louder still. With an intent glare she changed the final word to the lyrics, "*BLACK, BLACK, BLACK is the color of my true love's FACE.*"

"What's going to happen if daddy finds out?" she asked.

My friendship with Dom's sister Angela had been my only safe haven in Paterson. Even though I had broken her brother's heart, Angela remained my friend. Angela was an intelligent, fair-haired Italian American beauty. She was three inches taller and three years older, and we shared the burden of large bosoms. If it hadn't been for Angela's influence throughout high school, *Beowulf,* a medieval novel I was forced to read in freshman English, might have been the first and last book I ever read. Angela was my incentive to turn off the television and start reading. She took me to my first Off-Broadway show and created my first suggested book list: Camus, Voltaire, Ayn Rand, Gore

Vidal, Huxley, Salinger, Herman Hesse, Philip Roth, Eldridge Cleaver, Dostoyevsky, Ginsberg, Kerouac, Ferlinghetti, Steinbeck, and James Baldwin were but a few of the influences that began to shape me.

After high school, I managed to take a few night classes at Rutgers University Extension in Paterson, and had the added good fortune to have Louis Ginsberg, the father of Allen Ginsberg, as my English Lit professor. Learning that Allen Ginsberg came out of Paterson gave me hope. Louis Ginsberg was a sweet older poet who had been published in the *New York Times*, and he was very proud of his son's accomplishments. From Louis Ginsburg I learned that William S. Burroughs had co-written a novel with Jack Kerouac in 1945 while they were living with Allen in Paterson. Learning that these Beat pioneers had a connection to Paterson—and had gotten the hell out—gave me more courage to break free. New York City was the option that most of Jersey's cool cats took when they left home, but I knew that Manhattan would not be far enough to escape my father's eyes. I needed more than a bridge and tunnel; I needed a whole continent between us.

9

TUNE in TURN on DROP out!

In the winter of 1965, The Mamas and the Papas' lyrics called to me: *"All the leaves are brown and the sky is grey, I've been for a walk on a winter's day. I'd be safe and warm if I was in LA, California Dreamin' on such a winter's day."*

I would have followed the flower children to San Francisco, but I got waylaid by an offer to stay in L.A. with Elizabeth, my older Cousin Lucille's maid of honor. Elizabeth was a tall, beautiful, blond German immigrant in her mid-twenties. When she met my parents at my cousin's wedding, she promised them she would look after me like a big sister if I came to California.

It was a chilling, bone-aching Jersey winter when I boarded my first flight ever to Los Angeles, but I was without fear or trepidation. Although the tarmac was icy at the Newark Airport, I was all sunshine, wearing a pink and orange mini skirt with matching fruit-loop earrings and my pink plastic go-go boots, all shoplifted from Gimbels Department Store in the Paramus Mall. It hadn't been easy saying goodbye to my sobbing mother and teary father and sister as they watched me hug my little brother Richie goodbye.

It was January, just a few days past my nineteenth birthday, when my plane landed at LAX, and as I stepped out onto the shaky ground of Southern California, I knew that the promise of free love and peace along with the California surf was about to wipe out the guilt I carried for committing the crime of the century. The crime being that I was the first and only, out of all my thirty-three cousins, to commit the sin of leaving their parents' home before getting married.

Elizabeth resembled a neat and trim Pan Am stewardess when she picked me up at LAX with her German boyfriend Walter. They brought me straightaway to my new home: one of many identical apartment compounds located on Roscoe Boulevard, in the heart of the East San Fernando Valley and down the road from Budweiser, at the Anheuser- Busch Brewery.

Walter helped carry my luggage while Elizabeth, in her thick German accent, gave me a mini tour of my new surroundings. We passed through the courtyard that looked like a Howard Johnson Hotel with a medium-size swimming pool and entered a 1950s-style two-bedroom apartment with cottage-cheese ceilings. Then Elizabeth introduced me to her roommates, Gertrude and Elkie, also German immigrants and in their mid-twenties. All three women were blonds and towered over me by at least a foot. They told me they had met one another at the German Club in the Valley, where they also met their German boyfriends, and gave me a standing invitation to join them there on the weekends.

Elizabeth and Gertrude were engaged to Walter and Hans, and the two couples were exceptionally kind to me.

They would take me along on road trips to see parts of California European tourists lived for. We went to the Hearst Castle, and to Solvang, the Danish Village near Santa Barbara. I felt like their mascot as I attempted to keep pace with the two pair of six footers as they goose stepped through the Danish Village on a pastry-tasting expedition.

"Yah, the creampuffs are good," Gertrude said, "but nothing like the ones we get back home." So that I would not feel left out, they insisted I attend Saturday-night dances at the German Club, where I sat like a bump on a log as they and their boyfriends socialized with other Aryans in their native tongue, drinking beer and eating sausages. The only difference between my weekends in Paterson and in L.A. on the Rhine was the menu. I went from overeating Italian sausage and cannoli to bratwurst and seven-layer German chocolate cake. After a few of these social outings I began to get restless and knew that if I kept hanging with them, I'd never fit into my "Itsy Bitsy Teenie Weenie Yellow Polka Dot Bikini," also shoplifted from Gimbels.

I had left home to get away from watchful eyes, but Elizabeth felt obligated to keep me on a short leash since she had promised my cousin Lucille and my parents to look after me. So here at little Deutschland in Panorama City, the good German women with strong work ethics made sure I wasted no time in finding a job. Elkie, with whom I shared a bedroom, would make sure I was up and out of bed at the crack of dawn when she left for work. Each morning she would hand me the want ads and ask, "Do you have any interviews today?"

I enrolled at Valley Junior College in Van Nuys, and took night classes in Philosophy and History of World Religions, and in a week I found my first job working at a laundry. I buried my nose in my books, ignoring the endless blocks of strip malls and low-rise apartments along Roscoe Boulevard on the dreary pre-dawn bus ride from

Panorama City. It took almost an hour to reach my destination in Sun Valley where, by 6 a.m., I began opening bundles of men's dirty, smelly work and dress shirts. You can take the girl out of Jersey, but it took awhile to take Jersey out of this girl. At least at the laundry in Sun Valley, I was out of the freezer and out of New Jersey. After two months of this routine I was reaching my breaking point, so I decided one day to play hooky.

10

Surf, Sand & Sins

I couldn't believe I had been in California for four months and had yet to see the beach. I took several buses from Panorama City to downtown L.A., and then one more bus that ran all the way along Wilshire Boulevard to the ocean in Santa Monica. My first stop was Pacific Ocean Park, the gateway into Venice. I was immediately attracted to the funky twin piers with their colorful head shops, melodic wind chimes, and pungent incense wafting through the fresh sea air. It was a welcome change from the strip-mall Valley scenery.

I kicked off my shoes and walked south on the sand, imagining that I could run into Gidget, or Annette Funicello and Frankie Avalon in a *Beach Blanket* movie, but the atmosphere reminded me more of Atlantic City mixed with Greenwich Village. There were some leftover remnants from the days when this funky beach Bohemia was once a hot spot. Electric cars still ran along the boardwalk—which wasn't made of wood, but was a wide, cement sidewalk. There were no tourists so only the old Jewish folks who sat on benches outside the senior center at Navy Street used these cars. Later, I learned that poor blacks and Mexicans lived a few blocks inland in a section of Venice white people referred to as Ghost Town.

It was 1965 and this was the Venice of Jim Morrison of The Doors, but I was still naive about the massive cultural earthquake that was shaking all around me. As I wandered along the Boardwalk, I met Mark Anthony, a tall, dark, handsome gypsy who looked just like El Guyio from *The Fantasticks*. He was hanging with some hippies panhandling for beers under one of the Asian-style pagodas. Mark Anthony told me he'd just been released from jail and was homeless. Without giving me any details about his crime other than saying he was innocent, his unfortunate incarceration inspired compassion in me and it wasn't long before I was under a blanket in the sand, giving him what every released convict prays for. As he put me on the bus back to the Valley, he made me promise to return for the weekend.

When I showed up on Good Friday with my cashed paycheck, he asked for money, and took what I offered to rent us a room at the St. Charles Hotel. The place had been fancy in its glory days, but by then it was a Venice flea trap on the corner of Windward and Speedway, renting rooms for $3 a night to hookers and transients. With the rest of my cash, Mark Anthony bought a bag of weed. I had smoked pot only once, with college friends back home, yet after just two hits I opened my eyes and saw this guy on top of me for what he truly was, a loser.

Since it was Easter weekend, I opted to stay at the beach with him, since I'd already paid for our room and it would spare me having to join my roommates at the German dance again, and church on Sunday morning. By Sunday afternoon, we were almost out of dope, and I had run completely out of my money—except for my bus fare back to the Valley. When I mentioned I was hungry, Mark

Anthony said he would take me out for Easter dinner. An hour later we were at the Bible Way Mission, a storefront on Main Street just north of Rose Ave., sharing a holiday feast with the homeless and alcoholic members of the beach community. Still stoned, and, starving, we got in line at the buffet table with the less fortunate and filled our plates. It wasn't my mom's manicotti, but the fried chicken backs, wings and sliced white bread slathered with margarine weren't so bad. The only cost for the meal was that I had to sit among the ill-smelling drunks and listen to a short Easter sermon given by a young pastor who reminded me that Christ died for my sins.

Later that afternoon, Mark Anthony and I smoked the last of the weed at some party where we crashed for awhile; when I awoke, my knight in dirty armor was gone, and along with him my new twenty-four carat gold cross with a diamond-chip, which Mom had sent me for my first Easter away from home. Just like El Guyio in *The Fantasticks*, this grifter Mark Anthony stole my naivety. That Easter Sunday marked the day of early seed planting that would sprout into the Mary saga yet to be played out in my life. It wasn't the suffering Virgin Mary, Mother of Sorrow—my namesake—that was budding, but Mary Magdalene in her pre-conversion days.

11

High Risk

I gave up the long, slow bus rides for high-speed adventurous travel by thumb. Some of the men who picked me up between the valley and the beach were as dangerous as the ones I was en route to see. My casual sexcapades were escalating and I began to indulge in men like a compulsive eater at a free buffet. After a fast and furious fuck under the pier at Pacific Ocean Park, Bill, a Vietnam Vet, introduced himself. He told me he was a Gemini. In California I learned that your astrological sign was more important than your name. Gemini meant twin or two personalities, but I wasn't at all prepared for the complexity of this Gemini's character.

Bill took me to a party on the beach where we got high and then took me back to his room at the St. Charles Hotel. After an hour of gazing into his deep blue pools—a roadmap to trouble that had witnessed horror—we fucked gently to the hotel's clock radio playing "Lucy in the Sky with Diamonds." While cradled in his arms, I suggested we return to the party—and suddenly Bill pulled out a knife and started wielding it wildly in my face.

Bill said, "This is the party, sister. Don't you know who I am? With the shining blade inches from my face, I sat quietly and let Bill rant.

"You don't fuck the son of God and then think there's a party more important than I am," he said. "I expect nothing but devotion from my disciples and I'm prepared to keep you here forever."

Then he momentarily became distracted and put down the knife and moved away from the bed. With his back toward me, I scooped my underwear off the floor and slipped on my panties and bra under the covers. With Bill then peeing in the sink just a few feet away, I ran out of the room. I didn't turn to look back to see if he was following. I just ran as fast as I could down the three flights of stairs in my underwear. All my belongings including my purse remained in the room. With a pounding heart I ran barefoot for ten blocks along the Speedway back to the party, where I had met some friendly hippies. In the doorway I ran smack dab into another Bill, also a Gemini I had met earlier that evening. I told him of my ordeal and he took pity on me. Bill covered me with the shirt off his back and offered to escort me back to the St. Charles where he would confront Bill #1 and rescue my purse and clothes.

Within less than four hours, I replaced Bill #1 with Bill #2. Bill #2 was mild-mannered, clean-cut and lean, and lived in a small, charming apartment on Marine Street, a half a block off the Ocean Front. This was a huge leap from the St. Charles lodging. If you stepped out on his fire escape, you could see the sailboats off the shore and smell the ocean air and incense burning from the head shops on the pier. I spent several weekends hanging out with Bill in his apartment, enjoying the tranquility of beach life. He was intellectual and kept his nose in a book whenever we weren't fucking. During the few weekends we spent together, I never learned anything more about Bill #2 then I did on the first night of our meeting. He seemed indifferent to whether I came or left. He was the antithesis of high drama. He didn't appear to have other friends and never mentioned work, family or past relationships. We rarely even discussed the books he read. Eventually I grew bored.

When I learned that Elizabeth sent a progress report to my folks in a letter telling them about my reckless behavior, I decided to move out and found a room in Van Nuys with two college gals my age. My new roommates were both un-wed mothers-to-be and each at different degrees of knocked-up-ness. Trudy was almost eight months along and shared her house with Mary, who was just a little bit pregnant. Both gals were a welcomed relief from the judgment I left behind at the Rhine garden, and at Trudy's house I had a room all to myself.

I would have stayed with Trudy and Mary for the long haul except that after my first night in their home, I accidentally started a fire by hanging my bras on the wall heater to dry—and almost burned down the house. They were pretty forgiving, considering that Trudy's mom's new shag carpet was a goner and the house smelled like smoke and burnt rubber. They gave me a month's notice and said they thought it best to keep the room free for their coming arrivals.

12

Race Riot

Still without wheels in the city built by Detroit's car lobbyist, I snapped up an opportunity to leave the Valley to move closer to Hollywood, after finding a new job as a file clerk in the Mid-Wilshire/Vermont section of L.A. At the job, I met Tony, a black gay boy who lived with his sister Max. She had recently been discharged from the Army due to her unplanned pregnancy, and they needed help paying the rent. I was excited to find a swimming pool at the Machie Apartments in a black, middle-class neighborhood on Crenshaw Boulevard, just south of Adams Boulevard. I transferred my credits from Valley College to Los Angeles City College, a two-year college with a reputation for excellence in Theatre Arts, and signed up for African American History and Acting.

My higher learning was about to accelerate the minute I met Eugene Peace that fall of 1966. My eyes were glued to the tall, cream-colored black man as he casually bopped into my African American History class, sporting a gigantic bleached blond Afro, and took the seat right next to mine.

At the class break, it didn't take him long to let me know that he was a proud native Angelino, born and raised in Watts, and an open bisexual, married to Linda, a nineteen-year-old, blond, white Valley Girl/topless dancer who supported him and their beautiful one-year-old son, Troy, while he earned his Associate Arts degree in Broadcasting. As luck would have it, Eugene lived right down the block from The Machie Apartments, and he offered me a ride home after school.

Eugene took down the top of his shiny turquoise 1965 Ford Fairlane convertible and offered to take me on what he called "The Post Watts Riot Tour." He told me I could use the info for an extra credit report.

Over the loud bass of Sam & Dave's "Hold On I'm Comin'" pumping through his car radio, Eugene proudly described the sights like a TV announcer as he drove through his neighborhood with the breeze reshaping his large Afro into a six-inch-high flattop. At first glance I saw no signs of the ghetto I imagined. Watts was very different from the slums I knew back east. I saw no run-down projects, only one-story wood-framed houses with gangs of black kids jumping double Dutch rope or shooting basketball hoops. He pointed to one home with a dried-up lawn and said it was the one he lived in as a child. To my wide eyes, the only things that looked ghetto were the winos hanging outside the liquor stores on every corner.

Eugene practiced different announcer voices as he described the surrounding. "Right here under the shadow of the renowned Watts Towers is the place where my cousin fat Mable stole my cherry." I was surprised at how easily intimate he was with me. "Girl, I bet you didn't know that one of your Pisans from Italy built this monument," he instructed.

"Really, I didn't know Italians lived in Watts." I was impressed by the beauty of the steel girders that reached up into the smoggy sky with their mosaic-like patterns made of broken colored glass, pottery and tiles that gleamed in the hot Los Angeles sun. It brought to mind a poor man's version of Cathedrals I had seen on post cards from Italy.

Eugene liked to call me by my full name. "Dee Grosso, you know you don't even look like an I-talian. You look like one of mama's paper sack brown children. Girl, you know you can pass for one of us?"

"When I was little everyone called me Blackie," I said. "I thought it was my nickname until Mom told me it had nothing to do with race. She said that before I could barely walk I used to chase the neighbor's cat calling its name, Blackie, over and over. To encourage me, Mom would repeat the word Blackie every time I'd say it, so I thought it was my name."

Gene laughed, "Girl, chasing black pussy has never been my thing."

Wanting to impress him, I spewed on. "By third grade, projects went up in my neighborhood and my class went from all white to half black. Overnight, my sister and I were yanked from PS #25 and transferred to Saint Anthony's Catholic School. The only excuse for this radical move was that we needed to prepare for our first Holy Communion."

Eugene raised in eyebrow. "So they didn't want you mingling with "Blackie?"

From that moment on I spent all my free time hanging out with Eugene and his crew. That included his wife, Linda, when she wasn't shaking her perfect silicon DD titties at the go-go bar. Leon, a heavyset, large Afro styling queen, and Scottie, a renegade Baptist gospel piano player, were at the core of the pack. Then there was Joanie, an ebony prostitute with a large baby bump, who brought the name Peaches to mind, a character from the Nina Simone song "Four Women"; and Tachki, a half Japanese, half black, pimped-out gangster/drug dealer with processed hair, who wore a doo rag. They were all part of the furniture at

Eugene's pad. These new instant friends were all *ghetto fabulous* decades before the term was en vogue.

As Eugene and I shopped the neighborhood markets for party foods, our intimacy grew. "Blackie, girl, get mama some lean ribs if you can find some," he ordered.

In my skimpy, stretchy tube top, I'd lean over the meat counter in search of the best cuts to please him as I continued to entertain with stories from my past.

"Gene, did I ever tell you about the time I got my hair fried?" I asked. "My sister has natural curly hair and Mom use to take me for regular perms so that my hair would match my sister's. She loved getting attention from strangers who thought Ginny and I were twins. The last time I let her do that I was eleven, when the hairdresser left the chemicals on too long. I was so awkward with my new overnight sprouting boobies—and then I had a fried head of frizz. I managed to pull it all up in a rubber band at the top of my head and created something that looked like an Afro Puff."

"Girl, you were ahead of your time," Eugene said laughing.

"Ever since I met you and the brothers, I have a whole new appreciation for my big-ass legs. All those years I spent drinking Metrical and slapping my thighs together a hundred times in hopes they'd grow smaller was a waste of my time."

Eugene said, "Okay, Lady Chatterley, remind me to keep you away from the Bennies." He was referring to his drug stash of mini-whites, the street name for Benzedrine, that we had taken before we'd gone shopping. This was my favorite high, which he generously shared.

Life with Eugene was a constant party. His wife didn't seem to mind me hanging around; I don't think she suspected that I was falling for her husband. I didn't even know it myself. Linda and Gene treated me like a little sister. I went everywhere with Gene and his crew. We went to gospel concerts of the Clara Ward Singers, since Scottie was their piano player and would get us in for free. We had free passes to the Olympic Arena for the Roller Derby because Gene's friends were on the home team. According to Gene, all the big stars of the L.A. T-Birds were queens, and when they weren't in the ring tearing each other's hair out, they were in bed with one another.

This was true for the girls, too, according to Joanie, a bisexual. She'd saunter over and squeeze her fat pregnant ass close to me on the couch and say, "The girl team is all Lesbos too. Just wait till you see those bitches go at it; they're way more vicious than the boys."

I felt sorry for Joanie and her unborn child because she was in love with the baby's daddy. He was an older rich, married Jewish businessman who kept Joanie and their baby a secret from his other family. She let him, as long as he paid her rent and kept her in drug money. Joanie confused me. Whenever she got high, she'd go from sisterly to lecherous, with aggressive, relentless come-ons. It was those times when Peaches came out: "My skin is black, my hair is wooly. I'll kill the first mother I see. My life has been rough." I liked her, but when she got high she scared me. Her addictions to bad love and dope continued throughout the birth of her little girl and to a second child, a boy with the same father. I eventually pulled away from her since I could not bear to witness the neglect of these children and her demise.

I was seeing life through a black subculture and a homosexual's lens, and this lifestyle went beyond anything I read about in James Baldwin's *Giovanni's Room*. Gene's wife, Linda, was also different from any women I ever met before. She knew the score about her husband's bisexuality and somehow accepted it. But Scottie and some of Gene's other male friends were living on the down-low. A few of them had wives and children who would occasionally socialize with us for a backyard BBQ of chicken, ribs, and hot links. I never understood how these women could not see how gay their husbands really were. Perhaps they just did not want to see it. If you didn't look too closely, in the daytime, the backyard party looked like an after-church social, but once the wives packed up the kids and the potato salad and went home, the party would take on a different tone.

Out came the camp and drag, and by nightfall, the Supremes' "Love Is Like An Itchin In My Heart" would blow the roof off. Every tall, fine, black gay and outrageous queen from the 'hood would line dance wall-to-wall in Eugene's living room. I'd stand in the midst of all these hues of glory and bounce my little heart out to the Supremes or Marvin Gaye's "I Heard It Through the Grapevine" the whole night long.

Linda taught me a trick or two as well. It was under her tutelage that I became a topless dancer. I was having trouble coming up with an idea for my acting improv class when Linda said, "Girl, why don't you do a skit about a topless dancer, shy and frightened on her first night on the job? Then you can end the skit pantomiming your pasties falling off. I'll loan you a pair of mine." I got an A on the improvisation.

I was on my way to manifesting my father's greatest fears: I was becoming an actress. With the help of Linda, I found an agent who would book me at one-night topless gigs. On Monday nights I worked at the Classic Cat, Hollywood's most famous topless club in the Sixties, located on the Sunset Strip across from the Whiskey a Go-Go. Not only did I get paid to dance, but I was hired for my acting skills as well. Monday was amateur night at the Classic Cat, and when the emcee asked if there were any girls in the house that wanted to try out for the amateur contest, I came up to the stage pretending to be a little Mexican housewife, accent and all, straight out of East L.A. To the patrons, I looked like the real thing. Back in

Jersey I was Italian, but in Los Angeles, even the Mexicans took me for one of their own.

The emcee asked why a housewife like me was willing to take off her clothes in front of strangers.

"I'm here to get even with my husband, that *pendejo*! He spends all his spare time in these clubs and leaves me home with the kids. I'll show him."

The audience ate it up and cheered me on as I stripped out of my jeans and embroidered peasant blouse, down to my panties. I was pretty damn proud of my grand performance, and one night the regular club dancers took me along with them across the street to the Whiskey where the doorman let us all in for free. That night, Jim Morrison and the Doors were playing and we had VIP seating.

13

Kill Bill

By 1967 I was finally living the life of a real California Girl. I had moved into my own one-bedroom cottage on Lockwood Avenue, closer to L.A. City College. I found a steady part-time job go-go dancing while I continued my studies. The Cherry Patch, a blue-collar joint in Highland Park, is where I got to perfect the art of topless dancing. Mostly I tended bar, but for twenty minutes out of every hour I would leave the bar as a bikini-clad barmaid and take the stage. Off came the top that covered a pair of cat-eye fringed pasties. Pasties were mandatory nipple covers in those days and required eyelash glue to hold them over my large brown nipples. I soon became the favorite dancer since the Mexican clientele preferred a woman with a little meat on her bones over the scrawny blondes that were the usual fare in that dive. The only problem with my popularity was that once I came down off stage, I could only respond to their come-ons with "*Yo no habla Espanola.*" The men would accuse me of being some uppity Chicana who was trying to pass herself off as a Gringa.

The Cherry Patch is where I met Bill #3. I hadn't yet grasped the significance of patterns that were showing up in threes. I had lived with three German immigrants; and with three unwed mothers; and dated two Bills, both Gemini; and then Bill # 3, also a Gemini, showed up.

Bill Barkley was a welder and one of the few white guys to frequent the Cherry Patch. He came in every night after his swing shift let out. Bill really wasn't my type, but there was something about him that made me buy his rap about being an artist and convinced me to go out with him. Perhaps it was just that he was one of the few guys in the joint who could speak English, or maybe I was just bored. I recalled that Allan Ginsberg had been a welder in the Brooklyn Navy Yard before he became a famous poet, so I gave Bill #3 the benefit of the doubt.

On our first date, we went straight from the bar to my place after my shift ended. Before we started to make out, the sensitive artist/welder confessed to having spent the last ten of his thirty-two years in a Florida state penitentiary— one-third of his entire life in a maximum security institution. He never told me the whole story, and I was afraid to ask. I suppose I was trying to be cool, so I accepted his half-assed explanation of having been framed for an armed robbery.

Although Bill's past was a shocker, it wasn't nearly as frightening as the sight of his naked body. His lily-white flesh was covered from head to toe with tattoos. I had seen the ones peeking out from his shirtsleeves—the crudely carved prison inks of love and hate on each finger—but I wasn't quite prepared for the rest. These tattoos were not what you'd expect to see on a sensitive artist. They were crude and garish and depicted sexual acts, a total turnoff, but I closed my eyes and surrendered.

As Bill made love to me, I thought about the tattoo-covered Rod Steiger in the title role of *The Illustrated Man*, a film vision of doom and danger I had seen where Steiger's frightening character was covered in skin illustrations that came alive and told the stories of his past. I should have read the ink on Bill #3, but I was afraid to look too deeply.

By our second date, Bill asked me to move in with him. Less than a month before I met Bill, Eugene had left Linda and was sharing my one bedroom, and my attraction for my platonic gay friend was escalating into a full-blown unrequited love affair that was killing me. I could never refuse Eugene anything, and along with him came his temporarily homeless friend, Leon, followed by Leon's cousin, Beverly, a butch dyke. With Gene, Leon and Beverly combing their Afros with my forks and taking over my tiny space, Bill was just one more added attraction to the three-ring circus. So when Bill invited me to live like a grownup in a relationship at a new location, I said yes. It seemed like a logical solution. I realized the impossibility of ever having Eugene all to myself, and this pushed me from the fast track on Soul Train to a furnished one bedroom near Paramount Studios off Gower Street. I was moving quicker than the Freeway Flyer had taken me from Van Nuys to downtown L.A.

Yippee, I was living in Hollywood! Bill got the place rent-free because the landlord wanted a married couple on the premises to manage and collect the rents. Our new honeymoon flat was one of twenty units in a rundown building on Gregory Street, and the tenants were an assortment of fruits and canned nuts: potheads, pill poppers, speed freaks, junkies and alcoholics. I, the fake Mrs. Bill Barkley, would be their new landlady. Bill Barkley, my artist, was revealing himself to be an artist of the con.

Our flat on the ground floor, like all the others, had originally been a large single, but a fake knotty-pine wall divider had been added to create a tiny bedroom barely large enough for a double bed. It was furnished with a fake knotty-pine dresser and end tables, and the windows were covered with pink plastic shower curtains in lieu of real blinds or drapes. On the day we moved in, Bill dropped me at the curb with all my possessions and then went back to his place to pick up his belongings. Upon his return I learned that not only was I to be the manageress, but I was also to be the mother of Maurice, his gigantic Weimaraner. I had never lived with a dog so, at first, Maurice frightened me. Bill hung his one and only piece of artwork over our bed: a watercolor portrait of Joan Baez that he had done while in prison. And on the dresser he displayed another surprise: his rare collection of Nazi daggers.

On that first day in our new place, Bill went to work and left me alone with the dog. I stayed up on the bed the rest of the afternoon to keep Maurice from jumping on me. On the stereo Dylan sang, "Lay Lady Lay, Lay upon your big brass bed" while I tried to get comfortable on the lumpy mattress. I eventually fell asleep and a while later was awakened from a scary dream in which a dark shadowy monster was looming over me in bed. With my heart racing, I slowly came to fully realize it was Maurice, the giant pooch standing bedside, waiting to go out for his evening walk. At first I interpreted this monster in my dream as my fear of the dog, but somewhere deep in the recesses of my subconscious, I knew who the monster really was—but pushed the thought aside.

Now that I was officially Bill's *old lady*, he insisted I quit topless dancing. He said he would pay the bills and all I had to do was attend my classes at L.A.C.C. and spend the rest of my time performing landlady duties and keeping him and the dog well fed. Maurice would pull me around the block on his twice-daily walks, and I spent the rest of my free time babysitting the tenants, particularly Myra, a thirty- something Jewish woman who was disabled by MS and had a prescription pain pill habit. On more than one occasion she almost burned down the entire building by taking too many meds and smoking in bed. Myra was just one of twenty stories that lived behind the closed doors at the Gregory Manor.

The worst of the lot were the speed freaks that lived on the top floor. Once, in the middle of the night, with Bill not home yet, I had to go up to their apartment and confront them for making too much noise. With rock music blaring from inside, I practically bloodied my knuckles banging on the door until it opened. When it finally did, a double barrel shotgun in the hands of the tweaked out tenant was aimed at my face. I just stood there in the face of danger and told the tenant that if he didn't turn down the noise, I would call the police, and then I turned my back and walked away.

Even these moments weren't enough of a reality check to wake me up. While all this drama was seeping through the cracks of the thin walls and through smoke filled hallways, my own little tragedy began to smolder. One Saturday afternoon, Bill left the apartment for a pack of cigs and didn't return. By Sunday I started to panic, imagining that something horrible must have happened to him. I decided to call the police and report him missing. When Bill nonchalantly strolled into our apartment on Monday without an explanation, I tried to explain how concerned I had been about his absence and how I had made a police report.

Bill said, "You stupid bitch, don't you ever call the police about me again or ask me where I go. It's none of your fucking business. You understand?"

Then our lovemaking got weird. After work, Bill would come home drunk and high on speed, and then keep me up all night trying to achieve his orgasm way past the point of any pleasure on my side. On other nights he would bring his welder buddies home to party and expect me, the little woman, to rise from the bed after 2 a.m. to serve them beers and listen to their less-than-witty drunken banter.

On one such night, during my school finals, I made the mistake of not being congenial enough, and the next thing I knew, his fist knocked me up against the knotty-pine wall. I slid to the floor, bleeding from a broken lip. His buddies tried to calm his rage as I lifted myself off the floor trembling and got the beers out of the fridge. For the next half hour I sat there silently listening to his abusive babble about other women in the building he intended to fuck, until he passed out and his buddies stumbled off.

The morning after, I got up quietly as to not wake him and hurried to catch the bus to school. On the ride along the east end of Hollywood's Santa Monica Blvd. to the campus, I was preoccupied with the tasks of my day ahead. It was finals week, and I had two that day, first physics and then acting. I had prepared the role of Blanche in *A Street Car Named Desire,* by Tennessee Williams, for my final scene. I was playing Blanche, but looking more like her roughed-up sister, Stella, after Stanley Kowalski knocked her around. I used my pain to play the poor deranged Blanche to the hilt. At the end of the long school day, I took a few red devils I had stashed. These were heavy narcotics that I never took more than one at a time. That day, I took enough to numb the pain of all abused women in fiction or reality. I was so high on the ride home that, when I got off the bus and started to walk the three long blocks back to my apartment, I had to lie down on someone's lawn. I passed out and slept for over an hour.

When I finally made it back to the apartment, Bill was waiting with great remorse and promises. I was still pretty fucked up when he sat me down on his lap and started kissing me gently on the bruises he had made. He brushed my hair aside and said, "Baby I'm so sorry. I don't know what got into me last night and I swear to you that it will never ever happen again."

I wanted to believe him, but I kept hearing the words of my mother in my head, "Don't ever let a man hit you." I knew something had to change, but I wasn't sure how to make it happen. With the semester over, I got an invitation from Mary, my ex, short-lived roommate from Van Nuys. She had friends who owned a dude ranch in the High Sierras who had invited her and her little son to come up and ride horses for a long weekend. She asked if I would join her and babysit for part of the time, and she'd pay all our expenses. I really wanted to go since I had never seen that part of the state and thought it would be fun. I told Bill about the invitation and, since he was feeling guilty for hitting me, the timing was perfect. Bill encouraged me to take the much-needed break.

At the dude ranch, I began to feel like my old self. I was learning how to ride horses and enjoying the time with Mary, her friends, and her toddler, and tried to push Bill out of my head. Bill had found the number of the Ranch, which I had forgot and left on the dresser, and he called me on Saturday night. I was jolted out of my safe place, but when I took his call there was something hypnotic in his voice luring me back to him. He sounded on the verge of tears and was pleading.

"I'm so sorry baby. I miss you. Will you ever be able to forgive me? When you get home baby, it's going to be different, I promise. I'll make it up to you. Just don't leave me. I've never loved a woman like you before."

As if I had been given a suggestion by a skilled hypnotist, I forgot my fear and started to look forward to our reunion.

It was after midnight on Sunday when I arrived home. I anticipated a warm welcome, but when I put the key in the door and walked in, Bill was gone. I flipped on the lights. The apartment looked almost empty. I noticed that all of

Bill's belongings, including Maurice and the picture of Joan Baez over the bed, were also gone. I was really shaken. Once the reality of his lie and betrayal hit me, I put my bag down on the empty bed and went over to the mirror at the dresser. I watched my tears fall as I sobbed like a melodramatic soap-opera actress over this crazy man and then, suddenly, I woke from the trance and my tears stopped. It occurred to me that I got lucky, that the monster of my dream was gone and I had gotten off easy. I breathed a huge sigh of relief.

Two weeks later I got a call from a woman who found my number on a matchbook in Bill's pocket, who claimed to be Mrs. Barkley, his legal wife. She opened with, "Are you the bitch my husband's been shacking up with for the last month? I just want you to know that he's back with me now for good and if I ever catch you with him, you are one dead bitch."

"Excuse me." I replied, "I had no idea that Bill was married. You don't have to worry about me." The real Mrs. Barkley went on to tell me that the reason Bill had moved in with me in the first place was because she had thrown him out of the house—temporarily.

"Honestly Mrs. Barkley, I know your Bill is a catch and that more than one woman would want him, but I can assure you I'm not one of them. Besides, I already have a new man, and if Bill knows what's good for him, he'll stay away. My new guy is a Marine and very jealous." At that the conversation was over and I never heard from the real Mrs. Barkley again.

The new man I was referring to was Larry, the brother of Alan, my scene partner who had played Stanley Kowalski in acting class. Just a few days after Bill disappeared, Alan asked me if I would do my part for the anti-war movement by taking in his brother Larry who was AWOL and hiding from the FBI until he could make his way up to Canada. Larry was not a tough Marine at all but a short, cute and cuddly Jewish boy who had been drafted into the Army and was about to be shipped off to Vietnam. Like most college kids of this time, I was against the Vietnam War, but this was the first time I ever took a stand. I knew I could get in trouble for hiding Larry, but the minute we met, we became instant friends and I wanted to help save him. He was a safe harbor for me, too, after living with Bill, and it wasn't long before we became lovers.

No less than a few days after the call from the real Mrs. Barkley, in the middle of the night with Larry in my bed, the front door opened. Bill stumbled in with his buddies after work to pick up the party where he had left off. He still had the key and was so loaded that he acted as if he still lived there and that I was still the little woman waiting for him at home. When he saw Larry in my bed he said nothing at first, but then took me aside and insisted I go down the hall with him to his buddy's apartment in the building so that we could talk. My fear was instantaneous, but he was acting friendly and said he just wanted to explain why he had left me. Since Bill was twice Larry's size, and I didn't want Larry to get hurt, I followed Bill, and left Larry with the welders at my place.

The moment Bill used a key to let himself into the other apartment, and I saw that his buddy was not there, I was jolted out of my sleep state. Bill threw me down on the floor. I realized that Bill had planned this evening. He said, "Bitch, you think you can bad mouth me to my wife? I thought they were educating you at that college, but I guess not. It's time I teach you a real lesson."

He brutally pulled off my clothes and started to rape me. As he pounded away at me he kept saying, "I'm gonna fix you so no other man will ever want you." Just as he reached his climax, he sunk his big teeth into my left cheek with all his might. Like branding a piece of cattle, he left his mark on my face and then passed out on top of me. I lay beneath him bleeding and in pain for what felt like an hour, but it was probably only ten minutes, and when I was sure he was out cold, I wiggled my way out from under his sweating, snoring body. I grabbed my robe and ran down the hall. I woke Larry up and we left the sleeping welders in my place and took off to Eugene's, where he was still living in my old apartment by the college. Eugene took one look at me and threw on his clothes and took me to the emergency room for a tetanus shot. The next day Eugene, Larry, Leon and Beverly the butch dyke all accompanied me back to Gregory Street to confront Bill. When we entered my apartment, Bill was gone and this time he took my stereo and albums, too. I began to question my attraction to dangerous men, and along with each loss of innocence went more of my valuables.

14

Baby Love

With all my reality checks bouncing and the curtain closed on the 'Landlady of Gregory Street', I moved to Hoover Street with roommates I met through a notice board at L.A.C.C. I had no vision for a future, and like a fool who digs a hole to China, I had no clue of my destination.

I assumed it was a coincidence that I had attracted three men named Bill, all born under the sign of Gemini, lived with three unwed mothers, and once again found myself in a household with yet another unwed mother. My new roommates were a couple who brought to mind plantation days in the Deep South. Eula was a simple African American gal from Alabama, and her baby's daddy, Norris, was light skinned and as Uncle Tom-ish as they come. He could almost pass for white, and was embarrassed to let his white friends on campus know he kept a darkie hidden at home. He never openly admitted to being Eula's child's father. It was through Eula and Norris that I met the next player who would further shape my unplanned journey.

Reginald Vinson, an Afro-sporting Gemini with handsome Middle Eastern features, was a fellow student I met through Norris. Reg was married, and had a stunning four-year-old, bi-racial daughter named Laura. Upon our first encounter, I felt no immediate attraction to him, but I instantly bonded to his exotic, bright little girl. Laura had large dark eyes and wavy long black ringlets that framed her light complexion. She was Lena Horn, Ava Garner and Jennifer Jones all rolled into a child. Reg would drop her off for Eula to babysit while he went to school, and Laura nestled right into my heart. I sensed her need for female companionship and on the mornings when I was home, I could give her the undivided time and attention that her babysitter Eula could not spare with a demanding two-year-old daughter of her own.

At the end of the semester Norris threw a party at our house and Reg was one of the guests. Reg had barely said more than a few words to me in his comings and goings, but the night of the party he got real chatty and went on and on with details of his middle class Denver upbringing and his boring selected studies in computer programming. The more cheap red wine he guzzled, the more he began to confess his troubles and reveal details about his unhappy married life.

Reg said, "I'm only twenty-five and I have ulcers already. The grief my wife gives me on top of my job, school and my kid is enough to kill a brother."

I smiled and politely asked what he did for work.

I'm a full-time night janitor at a high school in Highland Park, and I'm carrying an almost full semester's load of credits. Half-flirting and half-complaining, he confessed, "I don't know how I get so messed up over you crazy white women? My old lady is a spoiled heiress whose daddy owns half of Miami Beach. She drinks and takes those funny pills and has no motherly instincts. I know she's cheating on me, too, but I just can't prove it."

Despite the large Afro, Reg was relatively conservative for an Afro American in the days of emerging black power. Before the party ended, we were making out under the blooming Jacaranda in the back yard. In the following week, he played hooky from his job and picked me up for our first date. Without red wine, he was awkward making conversation and we just drove around Griffith Park until it got dark. Once he found his courage, he parked in front of the rainbow fountain on Los Feliz Boulevard and, like an innocent school boy, hesitantly put his arm around me and asked if he could kiss me. After my last brutish lover, I found his shyness refreshing. I felt safe in his arms and liked him because I knew he was a good dad to his little girl.

I knew he was cheating on his wife, but I felt sorry for the guy. I figured he wasn't getting any at home, and thought I'd help him out. I didn't really think it would go much beyond the second date. Reg asked me to join him in Highland Park at the high school where he worked. I didn't mind because I knew he really never had any spare time, so I showed up at the empty campus after 8 p.m. He unlocked the back door and let me in and I spent the first hour of our date accompanying him on his chores from one classroom to the next. Once his work was done, he led me into the band room. He unlocked a big closet with one of a hundred keys on a chain and took out several plush velour capes that were from the band uniforms and used them to make a soft comfortable bed on the floor for us. It was kind of romantic. Right there between the drums and the tubas we made sweet crazy love. His lovemaking brought to mind a more innocent time of taboo lovemaking like in the church basement at Saint Anthony's with Dominic. Reg may not have been the first married man I had sex with, but he was the first one I ever found myself falling for. If it hadn't been for his race, Reg was the kind of guy that even my father would have liked. He was conservative, hard working, dependable and a good provider to his family, even if he was cheating.

Not long after our night together, Reg came home earlier than usual from his job and found his wife in bed with a gun-toting revolutionary who he had always expected was his wife's lover. With that, he did an about face and came directly over to my place. Within days he found a one-bedroom apartment just a few blocks up the street from the Hoover plantation, and we moved in together.

I immediately fell into the role of the good wife. Reg only opened up emotionally to me after he had had a few drinks, and my neediness for more attention and reassurance grew, as did his resentment toward his ex-wife. When he drank, he would spew all the venom he had stored up over the five years of their horrible marriage; but when he was sober, he had little to say. At first I didn't mind, because I could lose myself in playing house, cooking and sex, and the occasional social outings with other couples.

Laura was a dream to care for. Reg and his ex had no formal custody agreement, so Reg would take her whenever it was convenient for him, about once or twice a week. Laura's need for love and attention brought out the best in me. One weekend, when Reg and I had plans with his friends Bill and Harriet to see *2001: A Space Odyssey*, Bill offered Reg and me a hit of LSD to enhance the film experience. Reg, cautious about hard drugs, turned it down, but I accepted. I had tripped once before on a half hit, and had a very pleasant sensual experience, so this time I took the whole hit. Just before we left the apartment for the film, Reg's ex-wife arrived unexpectedly to drop off Laura and, after a heated argument in muffled tones coming from the hallway, Laura joined us.

In the dark movie theatre as I came on to the acid, I became aware of Laura's labored asthmatic breathing. I felt an intense connection to Laura and sensed the child's illness had less to do with her bad cold and more to do with the disharmony in her family. I spontaneously placed her on my lap and rocked her in my arms. As she fell asleep with her head resting on my breast, our breathing began to synchronize. From the film's sound track, I also tuned into the amplified breathing coming from the astronauts in hibernation on their mission to Jupiter. I made a profound connection to the breath, the life force within, and how the astronauts were being kept alive by Hal, the spaceship's talking computer. The LSD was opening my mind to a much deeper conscious connection to life, love and the breath, but as I watched Hal the runaway computer take over the mission and one by one snuff out the life of each sleeping astronaut, I had a glimpse of understanding that Hal was like an out-of-control mind. As I watched the horror fantasy without, I felt my own love and energy from within healing Laura's labored breathing. By the time we left the theatre, Laura's cold symptoms were completely gone, with no signs of her asthmatic breathing.

I had been living with Reg for close to a year when my brother, Richie, then eight years old, came to visit. My brother thought Reg was the coolest guy, especially when Reg drove him all around L.A. on the back of his motorcycle. Richie and Laura were just a few years apart, and we took the kids to see Disneyland, and the zoo and pony rides at Griffith Park.

On the Fourth of July, that summer of '69, Dominic, my ex-high school sweetheart, made an unexpected visit to L.A. and crashed on our couch. After a long day's picnic at Griffith Park with Dom and the kids, Reg returned Laura to her Mom's, Dom retired on my couch, and I put Richie to sleep in our bed. That night Reg and I made love on the bathroom floor. Perhaps it was the unorthodox location, or the sexy red, white and blue halter I wore to the park in the heat of the day, but something had ignited Reg's passion to a fevered pitch. From the start, our sex life had been less than explosive, but on that Fourth of July, we popped like firecrackers. In our excitement, we forgot to take precautions. Without a rubber to hold them back, Reg's sperm took off like young men in a three-legged race. That night, one of them made the race to the finish.

My parents knew nothing of my relationship with Reg or of any other boyfriends since I left home. Days before I put my brother on the plane back to New Jersey, I wrote a thoughtful letter to my parents explaining that I had met the man of my dreams, and we were in a serious relationship. I placed the race card as carefully as I could in the middle of my glowing description of Reg and told them that I thought they would approve of Reg if they gave him a chance. I put the letter in the mail.

While waiting for the reaction of my father, I flashed back on a memory that I held of my family at the drive-in movies in 1959, when we went to see *Imitation of Life*. In the film, Lana Turner's young daughter, played by Sandra Dee, befriends a girl at the beach who, upon first glance, looks like a white child, until the girl's black mother shows up. When Lana learns that they are homeless, she decides to take in the woman with her daughter and offers her work as her maid. As the light-skinned black girl grows up alongside her white friend, the perky Sandra Dee, she grows unhappy and at school begins to pass herself off for white. As she grows older she begins to deny her mother, the only evidence of her true race. As soon as the girl is old enough, she runs away, abandoning her mom so that she can pass in a white world. The heartbroken mother dies an early and unexpected death, leaving the daughter to regret her choices.

I watched my father caught up in this tearjerker, trying to conceal his tears, and in that moment I took note of his softer side and stored the information. Now hoping against hope, I prayed that my dad would apply that same empathy toward me.

During that summer of '69, the murder at the Stones concert in Altamont shook the idealism of the love generation, and the Manson cult news was about to explode and add a wave of fear and confusion to my high hopes for peace. On the same day my parents went to Newark Airport to pick up my brother—who stepped off the plane darkly tanned, with his hair grown out into an Afro and wearing a large Tijuana sombrero—my letter arrived in their mailbox.

When I called to see if Richie had arrived home safely, my mother answered the phone and said that they just got back from the airport and had found my letter. My mother, a true romantic, spoke calmly. "As long as he's a good man and if you love him, I can learn to." I was shocked at how easily she had accepted Reg. She didn't hear my dad pick up the extension in their bedroom. With the same intensity he used to hurl the red high heels at me when I was twelve, he roared into the phone, "You nigger loving whore, as long as I'm alive you will never see your brother again." I was silent. "As far as I'm concerned you are dead to us. Do you hear me?"

With that the line was severed between California and New Jersey, between me and my blood kin. I felt like Tevya's middle daughter, Chavala, in *Fiddler on the Roof,* when her papa turns his back on her as she pleads, begging to be accepted despite marrying out of her faith. Deaf to his daughter's sobs, Tevya walks away hollering, "This I can never accept."

15

Cold Cats

W hen I told Reg I was pregnant it became clear that our relationship would not endure the addition of a baby. In our tiny love nest on the hottest day on record in July, Reg's coldness made the air-conditioner irrelevant.

Reg said, "Just when I'm getting on my feet, the last thing I need is another baby with a messed-up white woman. You better deal with it because I'm not going through that again."

I knew I was the rebound girl, but I never wanted to accept it. This rejection collided with and compounded the blow from my own father. I was only a few weeks along and, ironically, had registered to take biology during the late summer session at City College where I studied a mammal's single-cell transformation into a fetus during the first six weeks of my own pregnancy. Miserable from morning sickness and the corpse-like man lying next to me in bed, it was clear that, once again, I had made a love match that brought a whole new kind of pain.

I was willing to have an abortion to hold onto to Reg, and that would have been an easy solution, but the day before my appointment at the family un-planning clinic, I decided to take a few barbiturates to alleviate my misery. During that year living with Reg, I had been relatively sober except for the occasional joint and that one hit of acid I took for the *2001: A Space Odyssey* movie. That night I popped two red devils, and before I felt the full effect, I decided to visit my pal Eugene for some comfort and understanding. When Eugene saw my drugged condition, instead of letting me cry in my beer, he reprimanded me like an old Church Lady, "Dee Grosso, you have no business getting high, girl, you havin' a baby."

"I aint havin' no baby, I'm having a fucking abortion," I slurred.

"Dee Grosso, that's the stupidest thing I ever heard you say, you ain't having no abortion, girl, you Catholic," Gene said.

My left arm automatically sprang up and joined my right hand to give Gene the Italian style fuck-you salute as I mumbled more curse words at his shaming, wagging finger in my face. Then I left in a huff. The next day when I woke up sober and well rested, Eugene's words kept replaying in my head.

I reflected on a girlfriend back home who had gotten pregnant and made a choice she lived to regret. Her name was Ella May but we called her Red. She was a Georgia peach and a Jersey tomato all rolled into one. Everywhere we went together, heads turned. Her natural strawberry-blond waist-length hair and Liz Taylor eyes gave her a choice of any man she wanted, but she had the misfortune to fall in love with Johnnie, a rat pack bad boy wannabe who treated her like shit. When Johnnie knocked her up, Red decided to carry the baby to term because in 1964 abortion was not easy to come by and it was still illegal. Johnnie made her promise to give up the baby for adoption or he would leave her. In desperation to keep her baby, she brought the precious little carrot-top boy home from the hospital for his daddy to see him, hoping that the infant would melt his cold, hard heart, but it only infuriated Johnnie more. Just a few months after Red gave up her son for adoption, Johnnie left her and Red never recovered from the heartache of losing her son.

In light of what Gene had said to me the night before, I decided to cancel my appointment with the clinic and gamble on Reg's reaction. At the sixth week mark, biology and the mothering instinct had taken over; I was in love with Reg, or so I thought, and I wanted his child. I fully understood his reasons for not wanting to be tied down with another wife and child, yet I found the strength to choose the child over him. When I announced my decision, Reg moved out. He still lived in the neighborhood and continued to come around from time to time, mostly out of guilt or to get laid. I replaced my attraction to danger with a new addiction to the pain of unrequited love.

Just weeks after the fall semester began, I decided to drop out and get a full-time job. I was hired as a 411 operator, but between morning sickness and the boredom, I only lasted for about a month. It was then that Eugene taught me about the benefits of welfare and Medi-Cal, so I applied for Aid to Families with Dependent Children. My false pride made me withhold the identity of Reg as my child's father, knowing that the welfare department would go after him for child support. I told my caseworker that I didn't know who my baby's daddy was, but the caseworker wasn't buying it.

"Miss Grosso, I find it difficult to believe that a young lady of your intelligence and level of education does not recall who she had intercourse with over the past three months," he said.

If this guy thought I was a young lady, I made certain that he changed his point of view. "How'd you expect me to know my baby's daddy? You think I keep a list of every John I fuck? I'm a whore." That stopped him cold and he moved on to the next question on the form.

16

Name Game

At the end of my first trimester, the morning sickness—along with the mourning over my losses—ended. I was shocked at the number of strange men that found me to be attractive as I began to show my pregnancy. I even took one chubby chaser, a cute Latino boy from school, up on his offer to alleviate the sting of my doomed affair with Reg. I started to have a new lease on life and began to take care of my health and body. After quitting the job at the phone company and getting my welfare checks, I had lots of time to read and prepare my nest.

Demian, a name inspired by a Herman Hesse novel, was the name I chose for the boy I was convinced I was carrying. Knowing that Reg already had a girl, I got the notion that a boy might win him back to me. I was so certain that I was carrying a boy that I didn't even think about girls' names.

Just two weeks before my due date, I found myself on a bus packed with students from Los Angeles City College.

We were headed north to San Francisco to march in one of the country's largest antiwar protests. To save money, the organizers of the march had found the cheapest charter bus company possible, and I spent an uncomfortable twelve hours riding up Highway 101 through the dark night, pressed against the hard wooden seat that felt like the same one Rosa Parks refused to sit on in the back of the bus. By dawn, the bus deposited me and my fellow protestors somewhere in the Haight Ashbury. I followed the organizers who directed the traffic in the crowd of thousands of young people from all over California. After the sleepless night on the bus and a quick pit stop, we began walking up and down the many hills of San Francisco for what felt like hours. The discomfort of the trip and the lack of sleep did not matter since I was high on the experience and excited to be taking a stand for my conviction to help end the war.

On that day in 1970, in the crisp bay air, much hope hovered. Mesmerized, like a child at the fair, the magic and colorful banners led me. One image caught my eye above all the others—a bright banner that waved high above a group of Latino Students. The letters, VIVA LA RAZA—Long Live the Race—represented their racial and cultural pride. I made a mental note of the word Viva; that, I thought, would make a cool name for a girl—just in case. By the end of that long demonstration, we were assigned places to stay with locals who had opened their homes to the out-of-town demonstrators. For the first time in twenty-four hours, I got to recline on a stranger's sofa. No sooner had I stretched out and let my body relax, I was overcome by severe cramps. Sharp pains shot up and down my legs from my calves up to my inner thighs and into my hip sockets. I thought I was having early labor pains, but it turned out to be a false alarm and only leg cramps caused by the weight of my eight-month-pregnant body pounding the pavement the day long.

A month later, two weeks past my due date, I began to feel familiar cramps again, but this time I was so laid back that when Reg showed up, I insisted we stop off for Chinese food on our way to the hospital. I had not yet had dinner and argued that it wasn't good to deliver a baby on an empty stomach. As I took my first bite, I dropped my chopsticks into my egg drop soup and doubled over with the sharpest pain I had ever known. When the pain stopped, Reg, sitting across from me looking as though he saw a ghost, watched as I inhaled the rest of my meal. With only a few bites left, the next contraction hit.

By the time we checked into the hospital, it was after 9 p.m. and the pains were coming about every ten minutes. Once examined, the doctor told me I was almost fully dilated but my water had not yet broken. At which point, he took out a wooden stick about twice as long as the thing a manicurist uses to push down your cuticles, and with the sharp, pointed end, he inserted it into my vagina to pop my water sack; then came a pain that made any previous pain seem like your average period cramps.

After pushing for seven more hours with no further progress, the doctor signaled, "Houston, we have a problem." I was then wheeled into X-ray for a photo shoot. I was screaming. Perhaps if I had not gone to the low-end medical clinic for my prenatal care, the doctors might have paid attention to my narrow hips and would have known a C-section might be required. So after two more hours of unnecessary labor while waiting for the surgeon, a nurse finally wheeled me into the O.R. where I was given an epidural that took all the pain away. Then the doctor made a precise slice: a teeny, weenie, bikini cut, and out popped a baby girl, just shy of eight pounds, with the shoulders of a linebacker. Another life had come to save mine, and I called her Viva.

After a week-long recovery from post-surgery complications in the hospital, I returned to my apartment alone with Viva. I had just turned twenty-four and found no congratulatory cards from relatives; I had no diaper service, no fancy car seats or baby buggies, and no family elders to help ease me into motherhood. The only practical gift I possessed was a second-hand stroller given to me by Eugene, which his son Troy had outgrown. Nothing short of a miracle kept me and baby Viva alive in those first few weeks. Within days I started to use the hand-me-down stroller as a carriage and diaper carrier. I somehow managed to hold my healing incision with one hand as I carried bundles of dirty diapers and a baby in the other. I felt I was a warrior building scar tissue over my wounds.

After making two trips down the flight of steps from my apartment to the street, I placed my sleeping infant gently in the rickety old stroller in the flat out, non-seated, position. I then put the large laundry load at her head and started the climb up the hill on Hoover Street to the closest laundromat. As I pushed my precious bundle, I didn't notice that both Viva and the laundry were slowly inching back toward the opened front edge of the stroller. As I struggled to maneuver the heavy load over a high curb, I didn't realize at first that my baby had slipped out the top until she hit the pavement. In a panic, I reached for her imagining the worst; I was instantly relieved when she opened her big eyes and just smiled at me. In that instant I knew the load of dirty diapers must have softened her fall onto the hard pavement.

When I had first heard Joni Mitchell's album, *Blue*, I took note of a song called "Little Green" that she wrote about a daughter she had given up for adoption when she was nineteen. In her lyric, a phrase jumped out at me, "Child with a child, pretending." That was me. Although I was twenty-four, I was still a child, running wild, and it took a child of my own to put a speed bump on my road to self destruction.

17

Back Home

An unexpected call from Mom came. "I never meant to disown you, but what could I do?" She sobbed into the phone. "I'm sorry. It was my duty to obey your father. I hate to tell ya, but I got bad news. If you ever want to see your grandma again, ya better get here fast. Not seeing that baby is killing us both." So seven weeks into Viva's new life, I used my welfare check to buy a coach ticket and Viva and I boarded the red eye to Newark.

Since my father's house was still off limits, my friend Angela, then a professor at Rutgers University and married, with a two-year-old daughter, offered to let me stay at her home. I hadn't even unpacked when Mom called and told me to come over right away since Grandma had taken a turn for the worse and was asking for me; Dad would be at work all day.

Angela offered to drive me, but I wanted to walk after sitting for hours on the plane. I put Viva in a papoose snuggly strapped to my chest and took off for the two-mile hike across town. With spring in full bloom I strolled through my old neighborhood under the shade of the maple-lined streets and took a detour past my high school. As I observed carefree teens hanging in cliques, smoking and gossiping, I felt like the past five years had brought me light years away.

As I approached my family's home, I paused on the stoop where I used to sit to put on my roller skates; the same pungent lilies-of-the-valley still grew. There were blossoms on the cherry tree in the back yard, and I could hear the chirping of baby birds from the branches above. I remembered how, as kids, my sister and I would place dead baby birds that fell from these nests into shoe boxes and hold funeral services before we buried them in the yard. My own baby bird, Viva, was sound asleep at my breast as I rang the doorbell.

I was uneasy as I stood on the front porch waiting, and when the door opened, I knew why. Mom had set a trap. There, in the doorway, stood my father. Suddenly face-to-face, we were both speechless. The shock was somewhat absorbed when my little brother Richie flew past Dad and threw himself into my arms, nearly crushing Viva, who was still sleeping at my chest like a hidden weapon. Richie took my hand and escorted us past my father who remained in the doorway apparently dumbstruck.

As I stepped into the living room, Mom and Grandma showed their surprise like bad actors in a melodrama making gestures to the back row. But my sister was completely overcome since Mom knew better than to tell her of the plot ahead of time. Viva began to stir and I removed her from the pouch. A big fuss was made by all— all but Dad, who kept his silence and distance while observing his family in action. Mom reached for Viva first, then Ginny took her and held her up, and Grandma gave Viva the mandatory seal of approval with a pinch on the cheek. As the flurry of baby passing continued, Grandma called Dad over to join us. As Dad inched closer to examine his first-born grandchild, I could see a battle raging behind his eyes. The sentinels between head and heart were in full regalia. It was obvious that Viva carried the Grosso bloodline since she bore a strong resemblance to my father. Viva had his dark, soulful eyes and his nose. He tenderly stroked her cheek. Her mocha skin was no darker than my own. He ran his calloused fingers over her soft, beautiful black ringlets, the same ringlets his son and other daughter—the obedient one—possessed. How could he not accept his own flesh and blood? That's what Mom and Grandma were banking on. Dad was not a monster; he just had some old ideas he needed to shed, and my mother and grandmother had imagined the sight of my child would melt his heart. They were right.

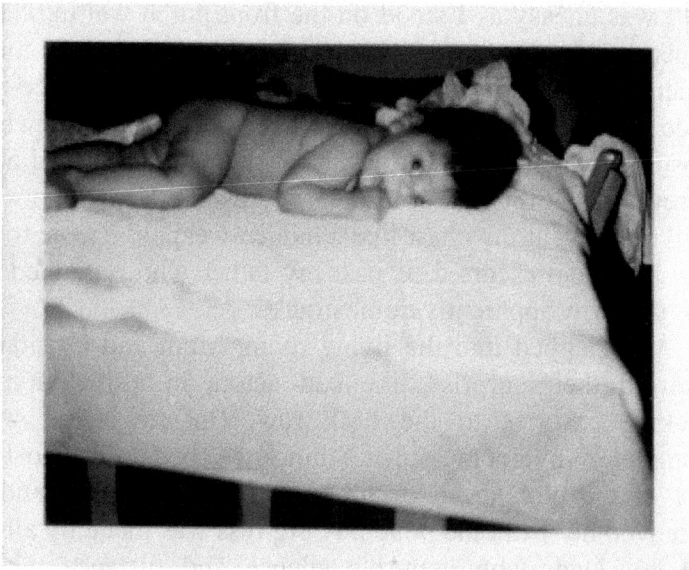

Viva at 7 weeks

"I made my special raviolis for you just the way you like them with the marinara sauce," Mom said. "It's about time we celebrate our first grandchild."

After being abandoned in the desert for so long, I felt like the prodigal daughter.

"Since I knew you were coming, I put a call into Father Mark and he said we can have a christening while you're here. I booked the church for next Sunday."

Mom was in her glory. She asked me to come up with a Christian name so that my child could be baptized in the Catholic Church. All the while, my father remained silent. Although I had rejected the faith of my youth, I was willing to compromise, and picking a second name for Viva was easy. It would be another version of Mary. Marie was my grandmother's name, so my child's full name would become, Viva Marie—long live my grandmother! It was the least I could do to repay Grandma for her years of looking after me. And this way Grandma, who had been diagnosed with stomach cancer, would live on.

When I took Viva to Mom's room to change her and put her down for a nap, I noticed the bed covered with dozens of homemade ravioli drying on towels over the bedspread. Jesus on the cross overlooked Mom as she scurried to scoop them up to bring them back to the kitchen. Mom took off with the dinner in her apron, and Richie and Ginny kept me company as I changed Viva and breast fed her until she fell asleep. As soon as she nodded out, I made a barrier with pillows to keep her from falling off the bed. Richie ran to his room to collect his favorite stuffed toy, the Black Sheep he had inherited from me. He wound it up and it played a lullaby.

Dad was out in the yard tending his garden, and I joined Grandma on the couch. Then Mom called us all to the table. At first, it was just like all the special family meals: everyone talking over one another; Mom scurrying about with her apron untied; Grandma and Dad yakking in Italian as the gigantic bowl of steaming ravioli was passed, followed by the cheese grater and extra sauce. We were only into our second course when Dad, out of nowhere, blurted out, "It's just not right for the races to mix; it even says so in the Bible."

Ginny attempted to make light of his remark and replied. "Dad, since when did you ever read the bible?" My father hadn't been in a church since my sister's wedding, never even owned a bible. But now he was interpreting the scriptures to support his argument.

Instantly the prodigal daughter's party came to an abrupt end. Like *Carrie* in the Da Palma horror classic, one minute I was happy and being crowned queen of the prom, and in the next I was hit over the head and dripping in shame and pig's blood. Mom started to cry as Dad made it clear that he was not going to take my defiance lying down.

"You have disgraced this family enough and now your mother expects me to invite my family to a Baptism in the Church, no less. How can you expect me to accept this child as my own flesh and blood? Even her own father doesn't want her? That poor kid doesn't have a race she can call her own."

I jumped up from the table, spilling Dad's red wine on Mom's best table cloth.

"Ever hear of the human race?" I yelled. Then I heard Viva's cries and I went to the bedroom to tend to her. As I got Viva ready to leave I could hear the drama escalate. Mom and Dad were fighting and Grandma was yelling at her son in Italian. My sister left the dinner table and offered me a ride back to Angela's house.

I stayed in Jersey for another two weeks and saw my sister, brother and Mom when she could get away. If this visit was my act of surrender, Dad was laying down the terms for the peace treaty. He had made it clear that he expected me to be punished for my crime. I went back to my little apartment in L.A. and my unrequited love affair with Viva's dad. My grandma died just a month after I left and I didn't return for her funeral. I rebuilt the wall between me and my dad, that went from coast-to-coast, and it remained for some years to come.

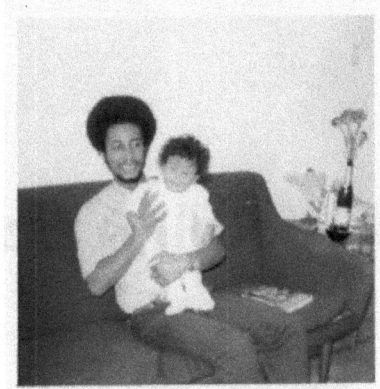

Viva six months old with and
Reg Vinson, her dad, 1970

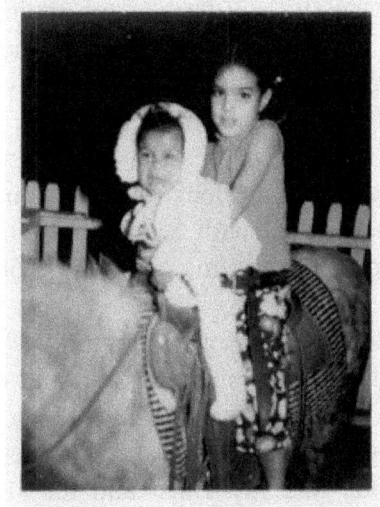

Viva's first pony ride with big sister
Laura Vinson, Griffith Park, 1970

18

Rock n' Roll A Go-Go

B y February 1971, Viva was ten months old and we moved to a small one-bedroom house on Navy Street in Venice, next door to Davy Jones Liquor Locker. After I put Viva down for the night, I unpacked the boxes of my meager possessions and set up my new kitchen. At exactly 6 o'clock the next morning, nature welcomed us to Venice with a magnitude 6.6 earthquake. Another pattern of threes: this one being 666—the symbol for the devil.

With a thunderous noise and ungodly shaking, all my dishes flew out of the cabinets. I jolted out of bed and ran to swoop up Viva and carried her outside into open space in the alley behind the house. My rattled nerves calmed when I noticed the sun had just risen and felt the magnificent warm, sunny, Santa Ana kind of day. Afraid to go back indoors, I buckled Viva in the baby seat on the back of my bicycle and off we rode along the Venice Boardwalk under an open sky. The clouds were tinged with soft pinks and the sky and ocean glimmered in its peachy glow. I passed neighbors I had yet to meet, all out discussing the shaker, but I just kept riding along. This was the same beach and boardwalk where I had plunged recklessly into deep dark waters less than five years prior and luckily came out alive. On that day, despite the disruption in nature, the glory of creation was evident; the mountains surrounding the L.A. basin were a vivid 3-D, and only peace and hope lived within me. These glimpses of a peace that surpassed human understanding made me fearless in the face of the unknown and the unsettling earth that rumbled with aftershocks.

I felt only gratitude that Viva and I were both alive, and that I had a joyful baby who sang at the top of her lungs, "la-la-la-la-la," from the back of my bicycle as I watched for signs of a tsunami in the calm waters of the Santa Monica Bay. "Sha-la-la-la-la-la, live for today" was my theme song, too, and Venice beach, the bohemian capital of southern California, suited me well.

Within months I began to earn my reputation as the hostess to the homos, and my little house was open to every hippy, commie, and queer on the west side of Los Angeles. There was always more than one person sharing my floor, couch or bed. I didn't know the meaning of the word anxiety and lived in the moment, grateful to be a member of the Welfare Elite. I had little ambition, and spent my nine-to-five on the water's edge with Viva and friends. It was a productive day if the laundry got done.

At this new juncture, even though I still saw Reg most weekends, many new men appeared to fill the role of baby daddy. A dear sweet boy named Bob Shomus moved in as a roommate but it wasn't long before he moved from the couch into my bed. Bob was a friend of Mary's from my valley days, and after his discharge from the Army and a recent divorce, he thought Venice was the perfect place to experiment with his new found bi-sexuality. He was also a good fit for me, not a hot and heavy lover but safe and cozy. We were instantly like couples who had been together for a very long time. The best part was that Bob was a natural parent and adored my baby girl. He would rise at the crack of dawn with Viva and take her out so that I could sleep in most mornings. Bob was slim and muscular and had a white boys' blonde Afro. He particularly fancied one of my stripper costumes, an orange suede loin cloth; he wore as his sun bathing suit for the beach. He would slather baby oil all over himself and slip on my loin cloth and then lift Viva up on his shoulders. Viva would hang onto his big Afro and he schlepped her down to the water. Somehow in that outfit, with a baby on his back, he imagined himself a man trap. Bob lived with us up until he met his dream, Wayne Masserellie.

With hindsight I know that this was the beginning of a trend I started for my love life. Bob was just the first of many self proclaimed bi-sexual men who made the leap to full blown homoville after sleeping with me. I was becoming the last stop at the station before leaving the closet for good. I wasn't jealous of Wayne but I did miss the intimacy I had with Bob over those few shorts months we lived together. Once Bob moved out and I stopped breastfeeding Viva, my self-destructive behaviors started to creep back in.

It had been like every other day under the sunny skies in 1972 when I carried Viva over the hot sand and set up camp in the secluded alcove, an impromptu nude beach where the gay community congregated. On this particular day, I felt a tremor on the shore when I noticed a young man rise out of the sea like a God. I was transfixed by his statuesque, toned, tanned muscles as they pulsated under the setting sun. In slow motion, like a model in a sexy soap commercial, he shook the golden drops of salty ocean off his glistening smooth, hairless flesh, and I sensed he was about to rock my world.

There were early warnings that this could be another natural disaster, but on the Richter Scale, Eric Smutz was a ten. I quickly learned that he was a Pisces, and a grand illusionist. From that very first encounter he began to spin a romantic fantasy—the one I had been longing for. Viva had just celebrated her second birthday and I had grown weary of the unrequited love affair I continued on and off with her father, who still had easy access to both Viva and my bed, though I made no demands for commitment or support.

I was twenty-six, and Eric was only twenty-one, and yet he quickly took charge of my heart. He never hid the fact that he was bisexual, and that he worked as a nude go-go boy at David and Goliath's, a Boys Bar in West Hollywood. I chose to ignore the signs that a union with Eric most likely would be a match made in Go-Go Hell. I myself had recently gone back to part time nude go-go dancing to supplement my welfare check. Eric told me that he had spent his childhood growing up in the high desert near Palmdale, California, where he began frying his brains on drugs at the tender age of twelve. The only other woman he had ever loved was his mama. These facts alone should have sent me running for shelter, but I couldn't see the landmines hiding all around me, and I just skipped right over them.

On our first date, Eric invited me to watch him dance naked in front of his adoring fans at David and Goliath's. It just happened to be amateur night and with a little encouragement from Eric I entered the contest. After all I was a pro, and since I was the only girl in the club, I could give the boys a taste of something that wasn't often on the menu. On stage, I began my striptease by removing the thick leather belt I wore around my hips and I used the belt as a whip. As I cracked the whip repeatedly at the edge of the stage, the boys went wild. I didn't know it yet, but I was building my future fan base. That night I took home the first prize of fifty bucks in cash.

A few days later when we were both high on acid, Eric proposed marriage, and on the way home from our date we picked up a hitchhiker and ended up in a three-way with him. For the next few weeks I stayed in a drug-induced trance, living in the midst of my carnival. Six months before I met Eric I had moved to a two-bedroom apartment on Horizon Ave. a few blocks south of Navy Street and two blocks from the beach front. I had two gay roommates and a nice backyard for Viva to play in. By the time I started to plan my wedding to Eric, we had eleven crashers and only my two roommates and I were paying rent.

My wedding was a perfect blend of Ghetto/California Hippy, with the ceremony taking place on a private strip of Malibu Beach Colony in front of the home of the parents of the young hitchhiker we had had the three-way with only a few weeks earlier. It was his wedding gift to us. My wedding gown was a long, white linen Indian import with lavender embroidered flowers down the front. My groom wore a matching see-through Indian shirt. We both wore flowers in our hair. Our rings were simple Santa Fe silver bands with inlayed turquoise stones, and our ceremony was facilitated by a minister with a certificate from the Universal Church of Life. I even catered my own reception, spending days cooking up vats of homemade lasagna for the affair, which was held back at my apartment in Venice. No one from the Grosso family ever R.S.V.P.d to my invitation, or acknowledged this marriage. This was no surprise, as I knew better than to expect gifts from this union.

The ceremony was captured on a Super 8 mm film by Butch Gorman. He and his wife Marie were the most normal people among my wedding guests. Marie was my sister's good friend and the closest representative to family from New Jersey and she and Butch had recently married and moved to Long Beach where Butch was attending school. The rest of my wedding guests looked like inmates from a mental asylum on a field trip to the beach. The guest list included my two roommates, Doran, a young radical faerie pot dealer, and Dorsey, a gay waiter; two nude dancers, Laura and Pam, from where I worked at Papa's Speakeasy; Eric's best man, Frank, the manager of David and Goliath's; Eugene, Leon and a few assorted queens from my old neighborhood; the unwed mother trilogy, Joni from the 'hood and Mary and Trudy from Van Nuys with their assorted children; my current Venice friends and a few students from L.A.C.C.; the groom's mother, a heavy set Puerto Rican woman; and Eric's two teenage sisters.

Reg also came along to babysit Viva during the ceremony, and he kept her over the weekend while Eric and I took a short honeymoon in Palm Springs. To his credit, Reg could see that another one of his babies' mamas was out of control, and he felt the need to provide some protection for his daughter. I knew that once I married Eric, I was saying goodbye to Reg for good.

Eric was a mirage from the get-go, so a trip to the desert canyon outside of Palm Springs was a perfect honeymoon location. Once there, Eric began to show disturbing signs of immaturity. Like Charles Grodin in *The Heartbreak Kid,* Eric became smitten with someone else on our honeymoon. In the movie, Grodin, a newlywed groom, is checking into a honeymoon hotel with his new bride when he spots Cybil Shepherd in the lobby and becomes obsessed with her. He leaves his wife alone in their room to pursue Cybil.

On our honeymoon, just minutes after we settled into the campsite, Eric spotted a hunky straight camper. But my *Heartbreak Kid,* Eric, shared his obsession openly and with lurid detail. Aware of the two-year-old waiting for me at home, I immediately realized I wasn't prepared to raise another child, especially one with special needs, so just twenty-four hours after the ceremony, in the middle of the desert, the mirage faded.

19

Lewd Nude

Viva was still at her dad's when I got home a day early from the honeymoon from hell, so I went to the beach alone to contemplate how to deal with my new spouse. At low tide, in the alcove of sand between the twin piers of Pacific Ocean Park, a mini nude beach was well hidden from the public, except for the occasional jogger who whizzed by. In all my wild worldliness, I still maintained a certain naiveté about some of the practices of gay males. I hadn't a clue that under those dark dank piers, boys were cavorting.

Rubin, one of my many good friends of these early Venice days, emerged from under the piers and joined me where I lay tanning in my birthday suit. Rubin was barely legal, a Mexican boy with long dark hair, smooth and hairless, and had chiseled features prettier than any señorita. As a young boy, Rubin had been abandoned by his mother and learned to fend for himself in boarding schools between the U.S. and Tijuana while his mother became a real-estate mogul in Tijuana. He maintained a slight

Mexican accent, and interjected the occasional Spanish word into his conversation. In exchange for my attention, Rubin was often at my side helping to lug Viva wherever we went. Less than a decade later, Rubin transitioned into Ruby, an outrageous transsexual who modeled her new full bosoms after my very own. But that day at the nude beach, Rubin was still flat chested. Rubin listened while I bitched about Eric.

"Girl, I thought I could handle an open marriage, but I didn't think I would have to hear about his tricks. It was like he deliberately wanted to hurt me," I said.

Rubin dropped the bib of his denim overalls and smeared my Coppertone all over his chest, "Oh *Miha*, I knew he was a Puerto Rican whore the first time I laid eyes on him. Just say the word and I'll help you mama. I got magic potions that can douche him out."

Suddenly from out of nowhere, two L.A.P.D. officers were standing over us. One cop barked at me, "Lady put your clothes on, you are under arrest".

"You have the right to remain silent," his cop buddy added.

"What?" I asked. I was in a daze.

I knew there were no laws on the books outlawing nude sunbathing.

"What have I done officer?" I asked.

"You are being charged with lewd and lascivious conduct."

As soon as I slipped my dress on, he slipped a pair of handcuffs around my wrists. Off I went into a paddy wagon, joining five lesbians I knew from the beach community. Minutes before my arrest, they had been swept up for topless sunbathing on Chi-Chi Beach, the official Gay Beach a half a mile down from the P.O.P. beach. The ride to the jailhouse was a hoot, with all us girls swapping stories about our arrest. At the arraignment, the judge recognized the absurdity of the trumped-up charges of prostitution. The arresting officers' report was an imaginative script that read like dialogue from a porno flick. The courtroom scene reminded me of old-time movies with bordello raids—but with a twist. With the exception of me, the rest of the bad girls were lesbian separatists. They would never even get near a cock.

"Do you actually expect me to believe that all these women were on the beach soliciting sex?" the judge asked. "There will be consequences if any other trumped-up reports come to my court in the future."

With the officers publicly reprimanded, we were vindicated and released.

I was arrested again only a week later, on my way home from seeing the Joe Cocker concert movie at the Culver City drive-in. I was with my roommate, Dorsey, and we had Viva with us. Still flying high from the music, at first I didn't see the all-too-familiar revolving red lights of a patrol car in my rearview mirror. The cop pulled me over for a broken taillight and after running a check, out came the handcuffs. It turned out I had several unpaid parking tickets along with a warrant for a moving violation for which I had failed to appear. Dorsey took Viva home, and I went to Cybil Brand, the woman's county jail in downtown Los Angeles. As I lay in a cell beneath the bunk of a woman who was in for attempted murder, I felt dread. I cried for the first time in ages; another chink in my tough-girl armor came undone.

Eric, along with other unwanted roommates, was still living in my home, pretending that we were happy newlyweds. Even though I felt uneasy in his presence, I had yet to find the courage to throw him out. With him working nights, and me dancing a few day shifts a week, we passed each other like ships in the night. When Eric wasn't out turning tricks after his work shifts, he'd come home and climb into my bed. He even brought home a new lover he was convinced was his other soulmate, and talked me into sleeping with the both of them. That's how unconscious I was, that I allowed this to happen.

I was back on stage dancing extra shifts to pay back the bail money Dorsey had loaned me. Papa's Speak Easy, the dive where I worked, was in Wilmington near the L.A. harbor. It was a grand watering hole, with Day-Glo murals all along the walls, depicting women in degrading positions. I danced my heart out with a continuous porno loop on a screen behind me, wearing nothing but my high-heel pumps and large hoop earrings, while at the bar, the hungry, horny dogs stared up at my pussy as they lapped up their burgers and fries. When my act ended, I put on a sexy pajama top and hit the floor to make nice with the customers and take their drink orders.

My day job at Papa's was so seedy that on most days I required medication to get through my seven-hour shift. On the days I worked, Viva was taken care of by an older neighbor, Ida, who ran a small daycare down the block. A week before my arrest, I almost got fired for taking acid at work. I was peaking and spinning on the dance floor when I caught a glimpse of the action on the porno loop behind me. On the screen, two girls and a guy were going at it with a vibrating dildo. I was so tweaked from the speed-laced acid that the stark close-up of the vibrator going into the woman's vagina brought to mind a horror scene of a dentist drilling very bad gums. It was so graphic that I started to laugh hard and couldn't stop. Twenty minutes later, caught in an acid loop, I was still cackling at the top of my lungs back stage. The boss gave me a warning and sent me home because my laughter was turning off the customers.

A few days later I was dancing to an empty club. At high noon, a scrawny redneck trucker entered the bar. So it was just me smiling down at the jerk, while he sat there scarfing down his gentleman's lunch and staring up at my crotch. Once I was off stage, the guy started to proposition me. "You sure are one classy lady and you can dance too. I'd like to take you out dancing sometime, what-a-ya say?"

I gave him the standard reply, "I'm so sorry, but we're not allowed to date the customers."

Even though he looked harmless enough, I sensed trouble. He smelled like an ashtray doused in cheap cologne, but I did my job and served his beers and listened to his rap about how much he wanted me and how much he was willing to pay. With each beer, I turned down his offer.

"You know, little girl, I could really show you a good time, I've got plenty of cash," and he pulled out a wad of bills and waved them in my face. "And there's a lot more where this came from back in my truck."

Without any *mother's helpers* to pick me up, the day dragged on and on, and every time I had to bring him another beer, he kept upping his offer. It had been a slow shift with few tippers, and with what he was offering I could easily pay Dorsey all the bail money I owed him. By 7 p.m., when my shift was over, the trucker was still at the bar, and he was wasted. I knew Viva was safe with Ida the sitter, and I figured it would take me no more than a few minutes to earn that extra cash I needed. I'd be home by eight. Allowing my need for cash to override my original intuition, I decided to accept his offer. While still thinking my keen self-preservation instincts were intact, I insisted we drive to his truck, where he stashed his wad in my car since he was too drunk to drive.

Less than ten minutes away from Papa's, he directed me to drive down a long desolate dirt road into a parking lot that looked like a graveyard for trucks. There were no signs of life, just rows of large hauling trucks. When I came to a full stop, the trucker grabbed my arm and started twisting it behind my back and with his free hand; he turned off the engine and took my keys.

"Shut up, bitch and do what I tell you," he said.

Dazed and terrified, I wondered how a meek, drunk Dr. Jekyll could turn before my eyes into Mr. Hyde, a raging psycho. "You whores are all the same. I saw you give the high sign to that fag back at the bar." He twisted my arm even harder. "You're going to regret telling your pimp to follow me."

"I don't know what you're talking about. I have no pimp. No one is following us," I protested.

"Well, we'll just wait here and see," he growled.

"Please don't hurt me, please, I have a kid," I whimpered.

He tore off my blouse and used it to tie my arms behind my back, then pushed me through the bucket seats onto the floor in the back of my car. I could have screamed, but there was no one to hear me, and nowhere to run. He left me lying on the floor of my car while he drove around until it got dark. For over a half hour, my mind sank to the darkest places. I envisioned headlines in my hometown paper, "Local Girl Found Slain in Los Angeles Harbor– Stabbed Forty Times." I tried to lift my head to see where he was going, but every time I did, his fist met my skull.

Finally he found an isolated location and parked. He climbed between the bucket seats onto the back seat. I could hear a dog barking in the distance, but heard no other signs of life. He tore down my jeans and was on me, hell bent on making me pay for all the bitches who ever did him wrong. As his rage penetrated me, my nostrils filled with the overwhelming smell of beer, stale cigarettes and blood. My jeans were around my ankles and he was anally raping me, repeatedly banging my head into the ashtray. All I could see was the face of my little girl, so sweet and innocent, waiting for me at Ida's house. If I died, who would love and protect her? In the middle of the horror, I heard a tiny still voice within me, praying for the first time since I had left the Church. "Hail Mary Mother of God, please help me!" In that moment I made a bargain with the

Virgin Mary that if she got me out of this alive, I would mend my ways.

He finally climaxed. It felt like he left all his demons inside of me. As he dismounted my bruised body, he began to transition back into the same pathetic drunk I had met at the bar. He was scared now and babbling like an idiot as he drove my car erratically back toward Papa's. "I know you're going to call the police on me," he mumbled.

"Are you kidding? What cop is going to believe me? I'm a whore," I said. When we were within two blocks of the club, at a red light he jumped out and ran like a thief into the night. I moved behind the wheel and headed for the Long Beach freeway, toward home and my daughter. It didn't even occur to me to go back to Papa's to get help or report the rape. I was amazingly calm, oddly elated to be alive. I found a pay phone and called Ida the sitter and told her I had a flat and that I was on my way back home. Ida said she would bring Viva to my house and put her to bed and wait for me there. I believed that my bargaining with the Virgin Mary had given me another chance, and that I needed to make some serious changes in my life.

When I got home, I found Doran, Dorsey and Eric all out for the night, and Ida nodding in front of my TV. I was grateful not to have to explain my fresh bruises to Ida, who headed out the door half asleep in the dim light from my TV. I went into Viva's room and saw my blissful child sound asleep. Grateful to be alone, I got into a hot bath to soak away the beating. Even though I wanted Eric out of my house, he had not yet moved, but was desperately trying to hold on to our facade of a marriage. After my bath, I climbed into Viva's bed and fell asleep holding her close. I didn't tell anyone what happened to me until the next day, and even then I made light of the situation, playing the tough girl, as if it was just a bad trick on a hard night at work. I buried the terror and went on with my days as if nothing much had happened.

Only two days later, after a day at the beach, I put Viva down for a nap. Suddenly Eric was at my side acting romantic. I was so accustomed to never saying no, I gave myself to him even though I was not in the mood. I had taken a quarter hit of acid earlier, and as soon as Eric got on top of me, I looked up at him and literally saw the face of the devil. I pushed him off, and right then and there, told him the marriage was over and he had two weeks to move out.

Post traumatic stress was not a term I was familiar with, but that's what I must have been suffering because the next day, when I was back at work and stepped up on that stage and began to dance, I started to see horrible images of men attacking and killing me. I didn't even wait for my shift to end before I got off the stage and quit. Quitting nude dancing and Eric all at once was the first step toward a major shift in my life. In the next few weeks, I saw very little of Eric. When he was around, his energy was dark and scary since he knew his days were numbered. One of my friends, Rob Weise, moved in temporarily to lend protection. Rob was tall and handsome and I shared my bed with his warm fuzzy body to keep Eric out. Rob was a heavy partier like the rest of my crowd, but he had a more mature rational sense than most. One day, while I was tweaked on acid and trying to clean house while complaining about all the freeloaders, he said, "You know girl, you really need to stop taking drugs."

"Who are you to talk? " I said.

"You have a kid to protect, I don't," he scolded. Initially I was offended by his remark, but I knew he was right. That week he played my bodyguard and helped me dismiss the free loading crashers, and made Eric so uncomfortable he finally packed and left for good.

20

Drug Cure

I began to wonder why I attracted psychotic, violent men. Despite Dad's occasional rage, he was not a violent man and I never witnessed any physical abuse toward women in my family. Growing up with my dad and a drama queen for a mother, I had plenty of material to fill hours on a shrink's couch, but our family didn't believe in therapy. Once, when I suggested to Dad that he might want to consider getting Mom some professional help after a nervous breakdown brought on by a tiny scratch on the refrigerator door, Dad responded with, "What-a-ya, crazy? There's nothing wrong with your mother, it's just her nerves."

The question of my frequent collision with violent men still begged for an answer, so just a few weeks after being raped, I dropped a tab of acid and went to see the doctor. In this case, it was Doctor John and The Night Trippers appearing at the Troubadour. Acid was cheaper than an hour on the couch, much more fun, and gave me keen insights that may have taken years of analysis to yield.

This particular night of gaiety was just what the doctor ordered. The evening started when Dr. John himself helped me and my posse sneak in at the backstage door after I told him I knew Wally, his go-go dancer, a former Cockette from San Francisco. It was a star-studded night in the small venue. John Lennon and Bonnie Raitt sat just a few tables away from our party, and later they joined Dr. John and other musicians on the stage for a final jam.

Even though I was tripping, I noticed Lennon so stoned that he could barely stand up without the help of Bonnie and a few other musicians. I could tell he was high on heroin, too, by the color of his dark, murky-green aura. This was the same drab aura I read on a friend who only days before had attempted suicide. Seeing auras was another benefit of taking LSD. Except for Lennon's and my suicidal friend's auras, most of the auras I saw were beautiful violet light colors that I often saw around Doran, my roommate who was, I believed, an angel disguised as a pot dealer.

I fretted over John Lennon's condition that night, but failed to take heed of my own drug use as I followed my merry gang of boys to a downtown bar that Dorsey had heard about, a throwback to a '50s hard-core S&M scene for the after-party. Spring Street in downtown L.A. in 1972 was a frightening neighborhood. The LAPD patrolled the streets on foot in twos to protect themselves. So there I was, flying high with ruby-red lips and big hair, balancing on six-inch platforms, wrapped in a Dorothy Lamour print sarong, when I was stopped dead in my tracks by the doorman of this infamous gay glory hole. He pointed to a sign overhead, "No Women Allowed." I indignantly informed the skinny bow-tied gentleman, "There is no gay bar from New York City to San Francisco that has ever not welcomed me." Acting like Bette Midler on Quaaludes, I pushed and strutted right past him and buried myself among the big, bulbous, leather-clad men at the crowded bar while my friends were left in my dust to deal with the doorman.

I saw instantly that this was a serious cruise scene, nothing like the light gay world I knew and loved. When the doorman and my friends caught up to me and began to insist I leave, I defiantly argued that I was going nowhere since I had just ordered a drink, which was a complete lie since the bartender had refused to even look in my direction. I raised my voice over the loud hum and told the doorman in no uncertain terms, "Your rules are archaic and besides, these two gentlemen seated to my right and left don't mind my being here one bit." I had sandwiched myself between two humongous, muscled gorillas, one black and one white, a massive pair of salt-and-pepper shakers.

They both turned and looked at me for the first time. Pepper growled, "Bitch, get your girly white ass out of here right now."

And his partner added, "I'd listen if you know what's good for you."

Their threats were so loaded with venom that I felt my bowels loosen. That night I learned the meaning of a new big word for hate—"misogyny." In all my days of cavorting with homosexuals, I had never expected to see such loathing of women coming at me full force in what I thought was a gay bar.

So off I skipped into the night with my entourage in tow. The rumor of my feminine appearance inside the bar had already reached the streets and when I came outside I was greeted by a small gang of drag queens and trannies cheering my brave feminist action.

"You go girl!" "How'd you do it, girl?" the ragtag queens hollered.

"They don't let me in there—and I still have my dick," a tranny added.

I laughed and waved to the girls and then spotted two patrol officers and marched up to them to make a citizen's complaint about the bar's discrimination practices. The cops took one look into my dilated pupils and one said, "Young lady, you are lucky you got out of there alive, don't you know we have one or two stabbings in there every weekend. I suggest you do your slumming in a safer part of town."

As I walked back to my car, I felt the accumulated emotions of what I had endured only weeks before and now this added assault by hateful homosexuals. This was a rude awakening. Up until this night I thought all homosexuals loved and adored women. They were the only men who made me feel safe. Darkness engulfed me as I chugged along the streets of Dante's Downtown Inferno when out of the blue an invisible energy field fell over me like a misty rain. Along with this protective shield came a voice from within and a message saying, "Fear not, there is nothing in this world that will ever harm you again." The voice was not the looming voice of a perceived God but only my own voice, a small voice from within, and it continued to inform me with authority. "The rape you endured was karma for a past life transgression and your rapist was someone you had harmed in another lifetime. Now the slate is clean."

I was raised Catholic to believe in sin and punishment—heaven and hell—but this idea of karma from a past life was something new to consider. At this point in my life, I did not follow any religion or spiritual teaching, unless you call taking psychedelics and *Hippie-ism* a religion. I questioned this inner voice that was speaking louder and more clearly than ever before, and in this visceral shield of awareness, the answers to my questions began to make sense. I had reached a new plateau in consciousness, but it took almost a decade later to understand its full implications. I was twenty-seven, the same age as Janice Joplin, Jimi Hendrix and Jim Morrison were when they bit the dust. But unlike them, by some Grace, I had survived what astrologers call my Saturn Return. Saturn, the planet of restriction that rules my sun sign Capricorn, takes thirty years to complete its cycle around the Sun. According to the astrological theory, when approaching the thirtieth year mark, around twenty-seven, many experience great adversity, and how one handles it will affect the next thirty years of their life—that's if they survive.

ACT II

THEN CAME THE FAIR

21

Born Diva

That same year of my Saturn return, I met two film stars, Jane Fonda, a descendant of Hollywood royalty, and Divine, an overweight queen from Baltimore who became the world's most infamous drag queen after eating dog shit in John Waters' film, *Pink Flamingos*. Both of these "politically incorrect" showgirls were instrumental in pointing me in a new direction.

When I told a few of the dykes on Chi-Chi Beach about my near-fatal rape, the story spread like wildfires fanned by the Santa Ana winds. Overnight I became the cause célèbre of male-dominated oppression. One of the more radical lesbians put me in touch with Donna Deitch, an up-and-coming feminist filmmaker. She was looking for interesting women with a story for her graduate thesis, a film titled, *Woman to Woman: a Documentary about Hookers, Housewives and Other Mothers,* and I had earned all three subtitles for her film. Donna jumped at the chance to make me one of her film's main subjects. Even though I had already quit my nude dancing job, she persuaded me to get permission from the owner of Papa's to use the club as a location for my scenes in the movie.

Woman to Woman opens with a shot of me dancing naked in front of the lunchtime clientele. In a review of this film, The Harvard Crimson wrote, "*Dolores Deluxe—a working girl—wiggles her way down the runway wearing nothing but a large pair of earrings and a big smile.*" That was me, the happy hooker dancing my way through an unseemly situation. In another scene, Donna encouraged me to lead a feminist rap session with a few of my fellow dancers. Backstage, wearing a stretchy tube top revealing my ample décolletage, I discussed the occupational hazards of my profession while gesturing with my hands adorned with rings on every finger. As I added my own soundtrack from the jingling bracelets up to my elbows, a reflection in the mirror behind me reveals the rathole backstage with boas hanging on hooks and two of my coworkers. Laura, a severely impaired narcotic addict, is having great difficulty holding open her double false lashed eyelids as she slurs her contempt for our boss, while Pam, a simple gal, who was still dancing naked despite her sixth month baby bump, is nodding in agreement. I had come to L.A. with a vague ambition to be an actress and lost my way, but there I was, starring in a movie.

The all lesbian/feminist film crew became my new best friends and I was often invited to women's political discussion groups. Cindy Fitzpatrick, the film's musical director, invited me to an evening with Jane Fonda, following her tour of Vietnam. I was so excited to be in this gathering of women who were personally invited to meet Jane and view her slideshow. In her lecture, Jane told us a story about how the Vietnamese managed to get through their long imprisonment and occupation by sharing their art through song and poetry. In the middle of Jane's lecture, I had what Oprah calls an *aha moment*. I realized that my childhood dream of becoming a performer had gotten lost, and instead of acting, I was acting out. Jane's words and images not only helped me identify with the plight of the Vietnamese, but I could see that I had been in a prison of my own making. My exhibitionism on that seedy stage at Papa's was just this poor gal's way of looking for a creative outlet. I thought I was doing it for the money, but even in that degrading environment I took pride in the fact that I was a great natural dancer who's only training had been those movies I saw in my childhood.

Viva with roommates Horizon Ave. Venice, 1972

Hippie Mama
Photo by Christina Schlesinger

Viva dancing with All Girl Band, Venice Mural dedication, 1972
Photo by Judy Baca & Donna Deitch, compliments of SPARC

Cindy Fitzpatrick and Viva at Lesbian Conference, 1972
Photo by Christina Schlesinger

22

Divi

During that same summer of 1972 I met Gil Robison, a photographer and student of the San Francisco Art Institute. Gil took Viva and me to San Francisco where I had the great fortune to meet the infamous Cockettes, a gender-bender underground theatre group. Gil brought me along on his assignments to photograph the Cockettes at the Palace Theatre for their new show opening, *Vice Palace,* starring the infamous Divine, already an underground heroine for her roles in the John Waters cult classics.

When Divine took the stage in her foot-high bouffant wig that sat inches above a human's natural hairline and her painted cat eyes, I immediately recognized her as my long lost alien mother. She commanded the stage as she vamped in a skin tight sequined gown trailed by a six-foot netted fishtail. Not that drugs were needed to enhance the splendor of these performers, but the small taste of acid I had had before the show seared the memory of Mink Stole, David Baker Jr., Scrumbly Koldewyn, and Paula Pucker and the

Pioneers into my brain for all eternity. I was completely blown away with every act that was a sendup to my Hollywood childhood fantasies. These players sparkled brighter than the glitter on stage and the stars in the heavens.

Backstage, after the show, I was introduced to Divine. She instantly opened her arms and heart to me. As he/she wrapped me in her hug, I rested my head on her artificial breasts, an oversized brassiere stuffed with pellets. Her fake tits felt more natural than most of the silicone breast women have today, and Divine's falsies eventually proved to be more nourishing than the formula my birth mother used to force-feed me.

The next night I had the good fortune to be invited to a dinner party hosted by Scrumbly, the musical genius behind the Cockettes, where Divine was the guest of honor. Scrumbly, handsome with shoulder-length brown hair and a paternal personality, made me feel at home the moment I walked through his door. He was wearing pants he made from patched swatches of '40s floral drapery prints that matched his drapes and slipcovers. His roommate, Janice Sukitis, was a witty New Yorker with an accent as thick as a Sicilian slice. She offered me a delicate floral bite as she nonchalantly passed hors d'oeuvres, in her birthday suit. Her straight, jet-black, waist-length hair was the only thing covering her as she aired out the worst case of flaring psoriasis I have ever seen. Janice's skin condition kept Divine and I from filling up on appetizers.

When Janice finally put down the tray and sat next to us at the kitchen table, Divine whispered in my ear. "Thank God these chairs are made of vinyl. It's easier to clean up that way." She kept me in stitches all night.

By the end of the night I was calling her Divi, as did her closest friends. Soon this cast of characters would become major players in my life. As bizarre as they appeared to the world outside their clique, I felt like I had found my true tribe. You would never know to look at them, but Scrumbly personified the good father, and Divine was to become a mother to me and Jan, my naughty little sister.

Only weeks later, I got a call from Divine, asking if he could come down and spend a weekend at my place in Venice with his boyfriend David Baker Jr., leading man in Vice Palace. David flaunted his rippling six-pack on stage and his ass that was modeled from Michelangelo's David.

"Are you kidding?" I squealed into the phone, "I can't wait." I wouldn't have been more honored if it had been the queen of England calling. This was Divine, queen of all queens, and she wanted to come to my humble home.

My roommate Dorsey—the straightest gay man I ever lived with—had an expensive king-sized waterbed and other possessions he was protective of, and told me he was a bit squeamish about the renowned dogshit-eating performer coming to stay with us. My first impulse was to say, "Girl, get over yourself," but to keep the peace, I assured Dorsey that I'd give Divine and David my room, and keep her largesse off his furniture, and then it was a go.

Divine arrived on a Friday night with an entourage: David Baker Jr., along with David's friend Lorenzo Clover, a serious classical actor who I was not expecting, and Lorenzo's dog, Little Brother, a scraggy mutt. I moved Viva and myself into our living room and put Divi, David and the two surprise guests in my small bedroom.

My bed was a tall loft built by my short-lived gay husband. Eric had recently moved out, but while he was still trying to make our marriage work I got him to build us a loft, but then kicked him out before he completed the ladder. To get into this loft you had to step up onto the windowsill and then jump from there. Each night the boys would have to hoist Divine up into bed, but no one minded because it was a communal love fest from the moment they hit town.

On the first night of their arrival, my hunch about Divine being family from another planet was confirmed. Within moments of walking through the door, Divi pulled out a thank-you joint and offered it to me and my roommates. Doran, my pot-dealing roommate, lit the joint and took a long deep inhale.

"Now be careful girls, this is no ordinary joint," Divine said. "This shit's been dipped in amyl nitrate." Doran's eyes rolled back in his head as he handed the joint off to me.

"I inhaled plenty of amyl fumes on the disco dance floor." I told Divine.

"I'm just sayin', hon; it's very different when smoked than snorted."

Throwing all caution to the wind, I took a hit. With a taste of rocket fuel on my tongue I was catapulted into the outer limits. Luckily the trip only lasted seconds because it was so intense that, had it gone on any longer, I may have never returned to earth. After that one little taste, my human DNA was seriously rearranged and the deal was sealed. Divine and I were bonded through all eternity.

Divine also fell in love with her cosmic grandchild, Viva, when she saw my two-year-old modeling a new bunny fur coat I had bought her.

"Give me that fur coat, Girl!" Divine said.

"No way, lady, it will never fit you," Viva said.

Pot dealer Doran and drag-phobic Dorsey also fell for Divine's charm, and she adored them as well, along with the beach and my authentic Italian lasagna. All three guests and the dog had come for the weekend and ended up staying for over a month.

In the '70s, Venice was the Riviera for the Welfare Elite, and it offered the homosexual community a gay alternative to the cold foggy summers of San Francisco. Divine and David decided they needed a home in a warmer climate and began to search for a place of their own, while the party raged on at my place. I would cook pasta meals to feed an army, and Divine would bake individual pies for every single guest. Divine was the mother I always wished I had, all fun and games, and she kept her drama on the stage. She had the wit of Noël Coward, and was even funnier off stage than on.

Every day of that Indian summer, Divine in her velour Mumu and me in my hand-crocheted bikini would tote Viva down to the beach. He would keep the boys in stitches with dish about the Cockettes.

"Oh please, girl, that Sylvester, if it weren't for me, she wouldn't even have a career," he would say. "She can't sing. I have to stand behind the curtain for every show and when she needs to hit a high note, I'd have to stick her in the ass with my hat pin."

Divine would challenge other homosexuals to have chicken fights in the crashing waves and like kids romping in a public pool, he would lift me up on his large shoulders and we played against our opponents. There were never any strong-enough fags to knock us over. I was having the childhood I never had, an endless summer, all fun, all day at the beach, and party all night at the house.

On cold or cloudy days when Viva was at pre-school, I'd accompany Divine on visits to friends from Baltimore who now lived in Venice. One of his friends was the major Angel Dust dealer for the entire beachfront, ironically named Marty Sober. In the middle of the day after one or two puffs of this PCP, I'd find myself dancing like a rubber chicken with Divine in the dealer's dark basement apartment off of Ocean Avenue.

On one of these dust trips I recall having a three-way with David Baker and another friend named Rodney, while Divi sat on the floor next to us eating potato chips and watching us and television. My memories of that night were of Divine's laughter and the soft silky texture of David's skin. During these sexual experimentations, I was like a kid exploring the playground and felt no guilt or shame, and Divine never seemed jealous of my love for her David. Like a good mother, she loved us both unconditionally.

During that month, when Viva's dad took her for a weekend, David loaded his VW van with our Divine family and we headed south for a quick trip to Tijuana with a stopover in Laguna Beach. David's ex-boyfriend, Bart, now lived in Laguna with a new lover. The two men had corporate jobs and owned a lush hillside red-tiled, Spanish-style home overlooking the ocean. Bart had left a key for David under the mat in case he arrived before Bart got home from work. Bart was only expecting David, and David never told us that we hadn't been invited. Mid afternoon, just as we pulled into town, it started to rain, so instead of hitting the beach as planned, we went to the market and stocked up on groceries to make dinner for ourselves and our hosts.

Like social terrorists in a John Waters movie, we settled into our new temporary digs. Divine and I took ownership of the ultra-modern showroom kitchen. He began by taking down every one of their gleaming cooper pots that were hanging from hooks on the ceiling. We commenced to make culinary magic and a grand mess in the house that looked barely lived in. We felt completely at home, drinking cocktails as we cooked. We baked our signature dishes, lasagna and southern fried chicken. As mama Divi and I ruled the kitchen, the boys were playing all their great showtune albums on their fabulous sound system at top volume. It was grey and rainy outside, but inside the sun was shining. With flour flying and grease splattering all over the granite counter tops, Divine kept repeating, "Girl, these are some clean queens," and we laughed.

A little after five in the afternoon when the clean queens got home, they found that aliens had taken over their home. David introduced us. With strained horror the two men, buttoned up in corporate suits and ties, excused themselves to their bedroom to argue. When they came out, they announced they had previous plans for dinner. Divine graciously offered to save them some dessert. "Do you like pie? I baked a few."

Bart's lover Barry looked Divine up and down, "Don't bother, we are on diets." He stormed out with Bart fast on his heels. Neither one of them said that we had to leave, so we were left to enjoy their home for the rest of the evening.

After stuffing ourselves and having more cocktails and joints we all relaxed in the lovely living room. Lorenzo made a fire and he and his dog, Little Brother, cozied up in front of the fireplace while Divine and David sat at the large picture window on the couch. I sat in an antique rocker for hours crocheting a hat. As we watched the crashing waves on the stormy Laguna night, we sang show tunes until we got tired, and then we moved to the den to crash. Divine, David and I took the large guest waterbed. Before Bart and Barry left the house, they told Lorenzo to keep his dog tied up outside for the night, so Lorenzo put Little Brother on a long leash on the deck and slept out on the couch in the living room.

We were sound asleep when the homeowners came back, but were abruptly awakened at 6 a.m. when Barry got up and went out on the deck to get his soggy newspaper and saw the results of Little Brother's freakout overnight, tied up in the rain. The dog knocked over a few of the potted plants that lined the long stairway along the cliff to the beach. Barry's repressed emotions exploded in a rage against poor Little Brother and he kicked the dog down the steps. We woke up to cursing and Little Brother howling. Divine turned to me in bed and said, "Hon, I think it's time to leave." With that we grabbed our wounded dog and left the scene. Since it continued to rain, we changed our travel plans and headed north. Once back in Venice, the sun came out again and we resumed our endless summer on the beach well into the winter.

Toward the end of summer Divine and David found their own home—and a grand home it was, a palace off of Main Street behind the Bobi Leonard Interior Design shop. This shop was the only upscale establishment on Main Street at that time. The apartment's owner was an animal hoarder and kept over twenty dogs living there and let them shit all over the place. Before the owner agreed to rent Divine and David the apartment, they had to promise to keep her dogs. Somehow Divine convinced the loony landlady that she would take care of her dogs, and that's how they got the place. As soon as the ink was dry on the lease, one by one, the dogs started to disappear. It took Divine and David weeks to clean and sterilize the two-story place and paint it all white from floor to ceiling. When it was all done, it was truly a Vice Palace where the party never ended.

During that year, Goldie Glitters, another Cockette also living in Venice, started to make plans for her comeback in San Francisco. Goldie found Gary Bates, an L.A. choreographer and dance teacher at UCLA. He signed up for the challenge of directing a drag version of Cinderella, with Goldie in the lead, supported by the Cockettes. During the show meetings, always held on the beach, Divine suggested to Goldie and the director that they put me in the show because I was funny. If it had not been for Divine, I would not have become the clumsy Pumpkin that put me on the map to wonderland.

Me and Divine, show planning on Venice Beach, 1973

David Baker Jr. & Mink Stole in Vice Palace

Divine, My Alien Mother

23

Star Name

Since no one in my family ever grew much taller than five feet, I had good cause to change my family name. Grosso, the Italian word for big, to me could have only one meaning, FAT. I had even tried on the name of my heartbreak husband, Eric Smutz, until I learned that Smutz, in German, meant dirty. So big and dirty Dee had been recreated as Dolores De Luxe, and this stripper name followed me through my film debut in *Woman to Woman* and to my first appearance on the San Francisco stage at the Palace. That October in 1973, Viva was three and a half, and we temporarily moved to San Francisco for a month of rehearsals previous to the Halloween weekend performances of *Cinderella* at the Palace.

Unknown to me, before I arrived in San Francisco, my stage name had been appearing on a sign outside a small bodega on the corner of 22nd and Dolores streets, not far from Mission Dolores and lush, palm-dotted Dolores Park in the sunny Mission District. The DOLORES DE LUXE

Market was shining in large, neon, deco letters, and I took it as a welcome sign.

We crashed with David Pitch, formerly a beach neighbor, who now had a great apartment on Castro near 18th Street and was going by his new name, David Venice. David, a fellow Capricorn, had good Midwestern looks, a constant supply of drugs and an endless stream of young boys passing through the living room where Viva and I slept on his couch and matching love seat. We were barely there except to sleep. Most days were spent at rehearsals in a storefront on Valencia Street where Scrumbly lived with his piano and half a dozen roommates.

Scrumbly, the musical director for *Cinderella,* also played the coachman who pulled me from the pumpkin patch when I made my début that season. Besides Goldie Glitters and Scrumbly, I was getting to know Sweet Pam, Scrumbly's ex-wife, who was playing Cinderella's stepmother along with Pristine Condition and John Flowers, the ugly stepsisters, and Cockette Reggie and Joe Morocco, who were the dancing mice duo.

Being a single mom of a three year old didn't always fit comfortably with this scene, but at Scrumbly's, Viva and I were always welcomed, and we benefited from Scrumbly's paternal qualities. Scrumbly had experience with children, since he had a son with Sweet Pam that they called Cactus, and this made him sympathetic to my circumstances. He went out of his way to pay special attention to Viva, who didn't have it easy getting her needs met when she had to compete with so many adult children for attention. I recall that Scrumbly gave Viva a really cute cloth doll, and Viva named her Ms. Motherfucker. I guess that was one way of getting attention.

With the excitement building up to the Halloween show, San Francisco's brisk fall air was intoxicating on those days I spent in long rehearsals or shopping at Cliff's Hardware Store right down the block from Harvey Milk's

Castro Camera shop. Cliff's was more like a one-stop Five and Dime store where, along with tools, nuts and bolts, you could purchase the makings for fantasy costumes and accessories. In the fall, the windows were decorated with alluring items: bolts of fabric, boas and glitter, enough to make anyone gay. My new theatre friends also brought me to the Purple Heart Thrift Store in the Mission where you could find vintage drag in mint condition: furs, velvet and satin '30s and '40s dresses, and shoes for a steal.

Toward opening night, Divine came up from Venice to hang with us for the last week of show rehearsals and was constantly at my side. I'd often accompany him on daily visits to Hunga Dunga, a large commune on 18th Street, where Bobby Star, another Cockette, lived with a dozen other friends and fans of the Cockettes. Hunga Dunga had the best pot for sale in the city, and Divine used her celebrity to get plenty. She was welcomed everywhere, and since Viva and I went along with her, we met many members of the extended community.

On the day of tech rehearsal, Divine came to the theatre looking for me. The tech rehearsal had been going very slowly and in my boredom I ducked out for a break and ran into Mr. Chew, the Palace Theatre owner. For some reason I let Mr. Chew lure me upstairs into his office with a $10 bill. Next to the mimeograph machine that printed the first advertisements for the early Cockette shows stored in his office, I gave him a quick hand job. It was the only pay I received for my performance at that theatre. When I confessed my delinquency to Mama Divine, she let out a loud cackle.

"Girl, you're not the first to give that old *chink* a freebee. How do you think the rent gets paid on this theatre?

When the show closed after the Halloween weekend, I returned to my life in Venice. After that month in San Francisco, life on the beach no longer held the allure it once did. My attraction to show business pulled my compass north. Venice seemed dull by comparison to my San Francisco experience. Although Viva's Dad had offered no support, he was still spending most weekends with us, and when I told him I was considering a move, he voiced no objection. In some way I think he felt that by my moving away, he'd be off the hook. So just after my twenty-eighth birthday, and when Viva was almost four, we moved to San Francisco.

There were over one hundred communes at that time in San Francisco and my new friends homes were located between the Haight and the Castro and had names and distinct personalities and purposes. Rancho Del Ruby, the Hula Palace, Hunga Dunga, Mukluk Manor, Kaliflower, and the Angels of Light were but a few. As usual I had made no plans, and when I arrived in the city, I found out that there was no room at the inn for me and my child. Each household was filled to capacity, so I found myself dependent on the kindness of strangers.

A friend of a friend of a friend was kind enough to give my daughter and me his bedroom, complete with a large waterbed, while I searched for a place of my own in the Haight Ashbury. Being temporarily homeless with a child in the cold, "wet city" was unsettling, but despite the heavy fog tamping my optimism, I knew I had made the right move. After all, my name was still flashing in neon on the sunny corner of 22nd and Dolores.

Pristine Condition as Ugly Stepsister in Cinderella, 1973
Photo by Michael Zagaris

24

Show Home

I t couldn't have happened any faster or better if my Fairy Godmother had shown up and waved her magic wand. In less than two weeks, I found a four-bedroom railroad flat close to the top of the hill at Frederick on Clayton Street in the Haight Ashbury district. It was two blocks from Haight Street and four from Golden Gate Park. My flat was the middle apartment in a three-story Victorian, with the Robinsons, my landlords, below, and a few black jazz musicians who silently came and went above.

Mr. and Mrs. Robinson and their two daughters were a working-class African American family who had a great tolerance for the crazy kids who multiplied like cockroaches over their heads. Easygoing Mr. Robinson spent his days drinking Ripple wine and hanging on the stoop, while Mrs. Robinson, a respectable church lady, ran the show in style, coming and going in her fancy red Pontiac convertible with her name and astrological sign, Dorothy Sagittarius, painted in gold lettering on the side door. Her youngest daughter, Lisa, was the same age as Viva, and Dorothy Sag and her teenage daughter, Vanessa, served as convenient babysitters.

When I put out an invitation to my Venice neighbor, Jimmy Evans, to join me up north, he gave up his apartment on Pacific Avenue next to the original Gold's Gym. Jimmy, a slight, short blonde with long hair, had grown weary of being called "Little Man" or "Lady" by his larger-than-life neighbors from Gold's (the gorillas in the sand, as we called them) who came and went from the gym to the beach.

It was during this same year that the homosexuals of Venice were experiencing an escalation in police brutality. The LAPD was doing their part to sweep the beach clean of undesirables to make way for the city planner's new gentrified Venice of today. My friend, Rob Weiss, had been beaten by the cops as he walked home alone, minding his own business after leaving the Pink Elephant, a gay bar on Main Street. The Pink Elephant and The Rooster Fish, the other gay bar in Venice had reported similar events. This harassment prompted a mass migration of gays to San Francisco.

Less than a week after Jimmy moved into our new digs, he met Marshall Reiner, an elfish, Pan-like, Jewish, East-coast transplant who was looking for a place to live. Marshall, short with dark curly hair, was a perfect blend of East Coast Jew and Hindu Mahatma. Marshall was Woody Allen on Quaaludes—neurotic and laid-back at the same time, and I embraced him, complications and all. Whenever Marshall got too stoned, he'd get extremely anxious and crawl into my bed.

"Girl, please tell me I'm okay, I'm not a failure, am I?" Marshall asked.

I'd put my arms around him and gently spoon him and say, "Honey you're fine. Just take some deep breaths. You'll be even better after you take a little nap."

"Thanks girl, what would I do without you? You're my barometer."

Basically, Marshall was asking me to be a loving mother, so my mothering skills expanded beyond the immediate needs of my daughter.

With another pass of fairy godmother's wand, the four bedrooms, back porch and eventually the tiny space under the stairwell became useful as my family grew. Along with the adult children in my home, I was giving birth to a new surge of creativity and style. My new family helped me unleash dormant talents I didn't know I possessed—like interior decorating, for one. Before I knew it, each room in my home took on a different personality reminiscent of a Hollywood movic set, and the cast of characters in my play kept appearing.

At a party one night I met Mark America, a brilliant visual artist from London who spoke proper Queen's English, and I immediately cast him in the role of my set decorator in exchange for rent. Mark was easy on the eyes: gorgeous, blonde, and with a slim, fit, muscular build. After I told Mark that I missed the warmer climate back in L.A., he painted lush green tropical jungle murals of swaying palm trees and warm golden sunsets in the living room, to remind me of my sunny days on Venice Beach. All through that first winter he served me tea and kept me cozy with stories of his naughty days in British boarding schools. Mark, like Marshall, had his own brand of dysfunction. Although he grew up with a proper upper-class education, he had the qualities of an orphan boy like Oliver Twist in *Oliver*. He, too, appeared to be another motherless child, but he bonded well with his new brothers, Jimmy and Marshall.

In the thrift stores, I found exquisite '40s rattan furniture. My dear friend Scrumbly, a wiz at the sewing machine, whipped up slipcovers from vintage draperies as a housewarming gift. All this decorating was done on a dime;

I was learning quickly how to live like a queen on a welfare budget. Within months, I had a '50s red Formica kitchen set found at the Purple Heart Thrift Store. Scrumbly had told me about the Foster and Kaiser Warehouse in Oakland where I purchased an original ad for Hellman's Mayonnaise: a super-sized billboard poster of gigantic salad vegetables large enough to be seen in Oakland as you entered the Bay Bridge. We glued it to one kitchen wall and Mark painted the kitchen in primary colors to accent this miraculous find. Our kitchen resembled a fifties diner and was large enough for feasts and dancing. We didn't have a jukebox, but we housed the stereo in one of the kitchen cupboards. My roommates helped with all the chores. Cooking, cleaning, and jitterbugging often went on simultaneously.

In exchange for my bi-monthly prescription of sixty Quaaludes provided by Doctor Feel Good—which I paid for with Medi-Cal stickers—I got Nicky, another Venice neighbor and a professional paper hanger, to come up for a weekend and hang the vintage wallpaper for my bedroom. I had found the wallpaper in the dusty back storage area of a small paint and paper store off Mission Street. Nicky even covered the curved Victorian ceiling with the soft-blue and delicate rose floral print. At another thrift store, I found a flawless vanity table and matching chair. It had a beveled mirror like the one my mom had in her bedroom, that I loved so much as a child. I was given the name of a cheap upholsterer, who I paid about $50 to make me a white satin, rolled and tucked deco headboard for my bed. When it was all done, my bedroom was a glorious send-up to my childhood movie favorites. Propped up against that headboard featuring a thriftstore satin nightgown, I felt like Ginger Rogers waiting for Fred to sweep me off my feet.

Before long, Martin, a husky, long-haired, East Coast Italian waiter, stumbled onto our steps. I can't recall who brought him to one of our parties, or why he stayed, but once I got to know him, he felt like a long lost Italian cousin. Martin was the only house member who had little interest in show business.

When Marshall decided to travel to Morocco and Turkey for a few months, he introduced us to Jerry, Sylvester's back-up singer. Jerry was a flamboyant African American queen who wanted to sublet Marshall's room, and I was delighted to replace Marshall with someone so close to Sylvester, the first Cockette on the rise to mainstream fame. Jerry had hopes to take that journey along with Sylvester, and he added a new dimension of color to our house and liked playing the role of Viva's black daddy who was obviously missing from the picture. Reg had come up only once that first year, at Christmas, to see his daughter. Reg also gave me a Christmas present: his old, used Datsun, in place of the four years of back child-support payments.

After a few months, Marshall returned from Morocco with more exotic herbs and habits. He allowed Jerry to keep his room and he moved himself into a small cubbyhole under the stairway. We always knew when Marshall was in by the smell of beedi cigarette smoke wafting through the hallway, coming from his tiny room under the stairwell.

If you pressed fast forward on the comings and goings of roommates at Clayton Street, it would make your head spin. It started with me and Viva, and then came Jimmy followed by Marshall, then Mark followed by Martin and Jerry. At this point my fabulous housepainter Mark had moved out, leaving six on board. Jimmy, my only roommate without decorator tendencies, had the only room that looked exactly as it did on the day he first occupied it, with his boxes still unpacked. He spent most nights at his boyfriend Billy Orchid's house, and we often used his room for guests.

John Compton, the Bay Area's most famous male bellydancer, joined our ranks for a short while, too, and converted the tiny back porch leading to the back door off the kitchen into a tiny bedroom that resembled an exotic stall at an outdoor market in Marrakesh. He brought Jimilla, his six-foot-long pet python with him. I first spotted John on stage at the Renaissance Fair where he melted my heart as he spun in circles balancing a silver tray and sword on top of his pretty head. I lost myself in his seductive black kohl-lined, cobalt-blue eyes. John stayed with us just long enough to teach Viva how to belly dance. He would put the python on top of Viva's wild curly locks, and little five-year-old Viva posed like a young queen of the Nile, never missing a step, pivoting to the beat.

The only female besides me and Viva to live under my roof was Debbie Debris—Tra-La-La Trent. Debbie, a plump, attractive, hennaed, curly top, renegade Jewish princess, moved in when Jerry left to go on tour. She came to us from L.A. via Berkeley, via Marshall's lover, David Greene. Jimmy and Marshall championed Debbie becoming the next roommate, but I had my reservations. The boys found her quick wit and over-the-top antics amusing, and accused me of being competitive when I protested.

"I'd be happy to have another real girl in the house, but she's got no boundaries," I argued.

Before Debbie moved in, she popped over one night while I was holding court in bed with another guest, my friend Jamian Merlin, a fair, long-haired, skinny filmmaker. I introduced Debbie to Jamian, and before I knew it Debbie was auditioning for a role in his next movie. Although Jamian was gay, Debbie said something that triggered Jamian to boast about his oral sex technique with women.

At this point in gay history—or maybe it was just San Francisco—most of the gay men I knew defined themselves as gay, but many in practice were bisexual. Perhaps it was the drug combinations we took that allowed for such open experimentation, but often it was a matter of refusing to be put in a box. Many of my friends were radical hippy anarchists who even countered the counterculture.

Debbie, in her coquettish, sledgehammer style, demanded that Jamian prove his point.

"Put your mouth where my honey is!" she said.

Jamian took her challenge and offered to service the both of us.

"No thanks", I said, "I've got the flu, and frankly the thought of a threeway with you guys is making me sicker." But that didn't stop Debbie. She whipped off her baggy overalls, giggling, "Don't mind if I do." Then she threw herself across my bed, right on top of me, and spread her scull-crushing thighs to allow for Jamian's face to enter her nether regions. I literally had to wiggle myself out from under the two of them and escape to Viva's room to get some rest that night.

Once Debbie moved in, she continued to live up to her title, "The Mistress of Offense." Until then our landlords had never complained about our raucous behavior. Then Debbie took possession of the room facing the front of the building. One day she decided to clean her birdcage and dump the droppings out the front window where the mess landed on the hood of Dorothy Sag's precious car just as she was pulling into the driveway. Soon after that incident, Mr. Robinson came up to fix a leak. When he found no one home, he let himself in and got a peek into Debbie's room with her debris everywhere. Debbie had every article of clothing she owned hanging out of every open drawer along with piles of fabrics, paper and sawdust covering the bed and floor. Fearing there might be a fire hazard, Mr. Robinson entered the room to check the electrical outlets and, in the dark, he tripped over Debbie's objet d'art on the floor: a life-sized doll she made from a man's suit, stuffed with rags to make it look like a decapitated corpse. She had also placed a knife in its chest and splattered fake blood all over the shirt. Somewhat tipsy from his Ripple, poor Mr. Robinson nearly had a stroke.

Debbie brought live mice without a cage into our house, and her idea of sculpture was a cow's tongue she shellacked on a spike and placed on her mantle. The only battle I ever won over Debbie's impulses was over the mice that kept multiplying and taking over our apartment. Even the boys backed me up on that one, and we set mouse traps everywhere and made her donate the ones still living to a pre-school co-op in the neighborhood.

Over the span of the next three and a half years on Clayton Street, many of my roommates' family, friends, lovers and tricks spent many a day and night, up to weeks at a time, in our house. Amidst the scents of broccoli, garlic, marijuana and patchouli oil, a few old ghosts lingered in the long hallway, too. I learned from neighbors that in the '60s, two tenants had died of overdoses in my apartment, and apparently their ghosts were unwilling to vacate the premises. These invisible boarders must have appreciated my leftovers, because on a few occasions items disappeared off our plates accompanied by the flickering of lights.

One night when everyone was out at some big event and I was home for lack of a babysitter, I put Viva to bed and used this rare opportunity to take a long, hot bath in the one bathroom all six of us shared. I ran the hot water, adding lavender and bubbles, and the minute I climbed into the tub and relaxed, I saw the doorknob move and heard noises from outside the bathroom door. Thinking that Viva had gotten out of bed or someone had come home early, I called out, but no one answered. After a few repetitions of the noise and knob jiggling, I got out of the tub, and as I approached the locked door, the doorknob moved again and I heard a loud pounding that came with such force that the door actually buckled. Thinking that this had to be one of my roommates playing a prank, I quickly opened the door and found no one on the other side. I checked every room and found the flat empty except for the sleeping Viva. I was so freaked out, I climbed into bed next to Viva and lay awake until Marshall got home. The next day, Marshall found a friendly ghost-be-gone ritual in one of his esoteric books and used it to smoke out the pranksters. Marshall dressed up for the occasion like a Catholic priest and Sufi dancer. He even had a Catholic incense burner with which to burn the sage. As he twirled through the long hallway *speaking in tongues*, he filled the hallway with thick smoke—and it did the trick. We never had another incident with spirits again.

For this mansion in the Haight, with every square foot utilized, we paid only $37.50 a month each, and the only time we ever heard from the Robinsons was when the sink drain backed up and overflowed into their kitchen. Debbie loved to mock Mr. Robinson's yelling, "You's floodin' us, you's floodin' us," until we turned off the water. Despite everything they endured, Mrs. Robinson was kind enough to braid Viva's unruly hair, and from time to time on Sundays took her to their Baptist church and allowed me to sleep in. I returned her kindness by taking her daughter, Lisa, along with me and Viva and the boys to the nude beach at Devil Slide. Little Lisa, not as God-fearing as her mama must have hoped, loved to run naked and wild with Viva kicking sand over all the nude boys baking in the sun.

My queer companions were my teachers, heroes and saviors. We valued each other, our drag, vintage items, and our next show. We dressed ourselves and decorated our rooms in the styles and glamour of any age we fancied, from Renaissance courtesans to 1950s rock and rollers. We pioneered recycling, health and fashion trends, shopped at whole-food community co-ops, did yoga, and ate organics and tofu decades before it became trendy. We were living the life yogis have strived for throughout the ages; we lived in the moment.

Once a month we'd hold a monthly house business meeting at Mommy Fortuna's, a local greasy spoon on Haight Street. Just for fun, we called ourselves 'The Coffee Shop Coalition' and dressed like '50s housewives with our hair up in curlers, and wore housecoats and slippers. No one in the hood ever blinked an eye. This was San Francisco. It was the dawning of a new age, and I thought I had found Shangri-La.

Diva in her Kitchen, with Vegetable Billboard
Photo by David Greene

Diva Deluxe with Vanity
Photo by David Greene

Diva Deluxe Counterculture Dancer from David Greene collection, 'Andy's Donuts, The Center of the Universe'

Posing in Debbie Trent's Room, Clayton Street, 1975
Photo by David Greene

Diva Holding Court in Bed Clayton Street, 1974
Photo by David Greene

25

Free Dish

Although my household was not a true commune, we borrowed much of the political and spiritual philosophies of our time. For lack of a better name, I called our home Casa Del Grande Boca—"house of the big mouth"—because no one could keep a secret. Neighboring communes with higher ideals like The Angels of Light, Hunga Dunga, and Kaliflower created food banks and free clinics, lived on strict vegan diets and pooled all their resources. They did free theatre and gave free dance and yoga classes to the community.

We managed to share just about everything, but we followed no rules. When I learned that Kentucky Fried Chicken used battery-caged chickens that never saw the light of day, I swore off KFC, but, at best, I was a quasi-vegetarian. I personally drew the line on giving everything away for the good of the whole, and held on fiercely to my individual boundaries and personal rights to my stuff.

One night at the Angels of Light commune, I popped in during the home birth of baby Govita, who had just made her entrance through Angel Lenore. I found Ralph, a former Cockette true to his title, "Kitchen Slut," cooking for the clan. I sat at the long table and watched him sauté onions to a caramelized perfection in a gigantic cast-iron pan. Tony Angel, the proud new papa, delivered a bedpan filled with a blob that looked like calves liver to the stove, and as I congratulated him, Ralph began to cut up the mystery meat and ad it into the onions on the stove. Ralph then informed me that the bloody mush was the fresh after birth just discharged from Lenore's uterus and went on to lecture me on the nutritional value of the placenta.

"This is the only meat we can eat without killing anything," he said, and then Ralph and Tony invited me to join them for a new life celebration dinner.

"No thanks, don't care for placenta, it looks too much like the baby calves liver my mother force fed me as a child."

Asshole Consciousness—a vague philosophy that had something to do with avoiding toilet paper—was another practice of the Angels that I could never warm up to. I dreaded using their bathroom unless I had brought plenty of tissues in my purse. In the Angels toilet next to the commode all you would fine was a coffee can filled with water to wash your butt after a dump, and more often than not, there was never a towel to dry off with. The infamous gender-bending troupes the Angels and the Cockettes shared the same roots, but became a house divided. Hibiscus, the Cockettes' founder along with Ralph and a few others, split off from the Cockettes due to ideological differences and formed The Angels of Light. Hibiscus and his new Angels, rejected structure and rehearsals and were heavily influenced by Irving, the head of Kaliflower, a commune that swayed heavily toward the left. Irving wrote an editorial in the Kaliflower newsletter berating the Cockettes for their ambition to grow along professional lines.

"They started free and sold out to golddigger dreams of riches and stardom."

But even after the split, members of both troupes often crossed lines and performed in each other's shows.

Like me, other newcomers to this community were the gang who lived at The Rancho Del Ruby. Their household mission was to flaunt decadence. Joe Morocco, one of my dancing-mice partners in *Cinderella*, was their charismatic leader, and his housemates included his lover, Doug, a Midwesterner, Janet Planet, and a few other New Yorkers who revolved in his orbit. They all shared a lavish, sprawling flat on the top floor of a Victorian on Haight Street near the corner of Divisadero. With the added benefit of a huge attic that doubled as a rehearsal studio, it made for a great party house.

The Ranch went through a phase when they converted from being heavy meat eaters to practicing a strict macrobiotic diet, juicing, and taking lots of supplements. This was not done for humanitarian reasons, but to counterbalance all the chemicals they smoked religiously. I myself had given up smoking the deadly PCP, commonly known as Angel Dust, but at Ranch parties, you would often find the guests so dusted on this animal tranquilizer that they stood like zombies holding on to the furniture and swaying for hours. For fear that someone would fall on her, I would have to hold Viva on my lap throughout the party.

One of their housemates was going through a plastic-art period and decided to throw a Tupperware party. Just before the demonstration lady arrived, Joe got everyone totally wasted on Angel Dust. I felt really sorry for the poor unsuspecting Tupperware lady as I watched her desperate attempts to get their attention and keep the rowdy gang from performing lewd acts with her merchandise. I don't think their original intention was to harass the Tupperware lady, but the Ranch considered events like these to be a living art experiment. As I watched the frustrated

Tupperware lady pack up and leave without a single sale, I knew it was cruel and inconsiderate. Because they were all so stoned, they didn't even consider the feelings of that woman. I knew it was not funny, and yet I chose to overlook their bad behavior because I was in awe of their creativity in general and wanted to be in the clique.

Another night at the Ranch, I attended a lovely sit-down dinner given to honor Janet Planet's new Zen master. The evening began with a six-course macrobiotic meal prepared by Janet, a Jewish girl from the Bronx with a geometric Sassoon haircut. Janet needed no drugs at all since even in her natural state she was always orbiting planet earth. By the end of the night, the dusted guests were standing comatose, holding up the walls and confusing the Zen Master. Later that night, after I left the party, I learned that one of the guests walked through a plate-glass door—and luckily survived.

No matter the show or the menu, Angel or Devil, Dust or Glitter, Dish was King, and in our community, it ran rampant. Joe Morocco appeared once in the Angels' Cabaret *Kitchen Show* wearing blackface, dressed as a pepper shaker singing and tapping to "Shaking the Blues Away." That night Joe Morocco, the dark knight, stole the show, and toward the finale all hell broke loose when, during the middle of the Angels' chorus number, Planet and Doug threw large chunks of raw ground beef on the stage where they were dancing to mock the Angles' strict vegan rules. From that day forth, the vile meat eaters were forbidden to work with the Angels.

These contradictions from light to dark behavior dominated our scene. I took what I wanted and left the rest. No matter whom we fucked or worshiped, what we ate, or how we wiped our asses, the one bond that held us together was the fact that we were all hams when it came to the stage, and we were often fiercely competitive.

26

Boom Boom

Janice Sukaitis, the naked party hostess I had met at Scrumbly's during my first trip to San Francisco, was the creative brain behind White Trash Boom-Boom, a troupe of chicks without dicks.

Theresa McGinley, Jan's childhood friend from Queens, came from a mixed-marriage—Italian mother and Irish Catholic father. Theresa could give Mother Superior a run for her money. Candida Royalle was an artsy, spicy tomato from Brooklyn and an aspiring jazz singer; and Lelani, a dead ringer for a young Marilyn Monroe, was seventeen years old and hailed from the Midwest. Like many of the wounded children in our midst, Lelani had survived on the streets since she was fourteen. Jealous of her own child's beauty, Lelani's mother threw Lelani out of the house when she discovered that her husband had been sexually abusing her daughter.

Janice, often behaving like little Rhoda in *The Bad Seed,* had little tolerance for complaints. She had a motto: "Use your neurosis, and write a play." Janice did that over and over again. Unlike today, where sharing personal wounds is encouraged by society and popular media, we buried our real-life dramas under crinolines and layers of hair and makeup. Like alchemists, we spun old hurts into gold on stages. Every show was created collectively. Someone came up with a concept and then every player put in their two cents until a script, lyrics, music, sets, costumes, posters and eventually a show was born. It was collectivism at its best.

In *White Trash, in Little Italy*, Candida, an art major, designed a simple cardboard set that was inspired by her neighborhood Brooklyn Italian Deli, with giant salamis and provolone hanging in the window. Like me, Candida, Janice and Theresa were recovering from Catholicism, and Jan wrote a clever skit expressing the perils of the double standard. Jan, Candida, Theresa and Lelani played the good Catholic girls. I was typecast as Gina, the town tramp who was stealing their boyfriends away because I was the only girl who would put out. We spoke all our lines with Italian accents. I can still see and hear sweet Lelani, dressed like a virgin in a white, pleated skirt and angora sweater, delivering her line to me in broken English, "But Gina, how-a you gonna get-a to heaven-a messin' around like-a that?"

And I replied, "Oh your Vito, he send-a me to heaven-a every night." The silly mini musical romp ended with all of us lip synching to a popular Italian song with lyrics we had no clue to the meaning of, but made up our own interpretation of.

Our stage for this one-night wonder was the bar top at The Stud, San Francisco's most popular gay bar, then in its original location on Folsom Street. Any night of the week you could count on wall-to-wall hot, hunky, long-hair hippy freaks, fags and hags packed in like sardines at this cruising paradise. With the scent of poppers, sweat and heat rising, we took the stage. We were San Francisco's version of Bette Midler at the gay bathhouses in New York, and the boys ate us up.

That night, when I got down from the stage, I was tapped on the shoulder by a long-haired redhead who looked vaguely familiar.

"Excuse me miss," he said, "but aren't you Dee Grosso, from Eastside High School?"

I turned with surprise to hear my long-forgotten family name, as he shouted over pumping dance music.

"I'm Marty Worman. I went to Eastside High with you ten years ago."

Martin had been a semester ahead of me. I soon learned that Martin performed with and wrote lyrics for the Cockettes. Martin was planning to put together a new troupe with some of the old Cockettes and some fresh talent and, based on the performance he saw that night, asked me and the other Boom-Boom girls to join his new company of performers. I was on my way to the big time.

The afterbirth of the Cockettes, Warped Floors was the new name our troupe decided upon after hours of arguing. Along with Martin, Scrumbly, Pristine Condition, and Bobby Star, this troupe was infused with a new breed of talent that included the White Trash Boom-Boom girls, Joe Morocco, Janet Planet, Jorge, and Liz Birsis from the Ranch, as well as Divine's matinee idol, David Baker Jr.

Scrumbly wrote all of the music, and Martin and Janice collaborated on the script and lyrics for this new musical. Martin, who had a master's degree in playwriting thanks to a Shubert fellowship, had been waiting since the original Cockettes had fallen apart to write a show with more serious political overtones. *Rickettes, a Day in the Life of the Counter Culture*, the first offering from Warped Floors, was to be the anti-Cockette production. No glitz, no glamour or glitter, and no big fake tits, please; this was a musical exploration of the plight of the humdrum workers who performed their duties at their counters in a department store.

I created the character Gloria, a wisecracking snack-bar waitress, based on my mother's heyday at the Woolworth's lunch counter. Janice wrote much of my scene, and Martin wrote me a brilliant lyric, "Tapping in a Varicose Vein," and as I sang the lament of the struggling waitress, Gloria, and her lost dream—"a fabulous dancer at Radio City, with three kids, I gotta to wurk"—I won the heart of my audience. And when I broke out into a full tapdance in my orthopedic tap shoes and support hose over varicose veins that looked like the NY subway system, with the entire cast tapping behind me, the showstopper earned me my first and best critical reviews ever. Unfortunately, some of my fellow performers were not so praised. On opening night, Lelani and Pristine had to be carried out due to Angel Dust overdoes. They came back to consciousness just in time for the bad reviews hit the press.

Boom Boom Girls in Little Italy, on the bar top at The Stud, 1974
Left to right: Lelani, Jan Sukaitis, Candida Royalle and me

27

Dild-O-Daze

That same year, *Rollover Alice* was another hit show happening around town. To build buzz for their new show, the Rollover Alice Company offered a free show in Golden Gate Park. They put the word out to the theatrical community at large to enter a special contest called "Queen of the Prom." This event would be woven into their show leading up to the intermission.

To enter the contest all one needed was a theme and an un-motorized float. For my shtick, I came up with *A Leather Queen's Wet Dream in the Castro*, and convinced my roommates to play my slaves. Mark America built the float out of a shopping cart and a large trash can. Then he fashioned the head of a giant dildo with chicken wire and paper mache. He painted the whole thing glossy black to create a twelve-foot-long black shiny penis contraption on wheels. We hid in the bushes, oiling our flesh and getting ready, so as not to spoil the impact of our entrance. The boys wore black thongs and heavy metal paraphernalia and were harnessed to my chariot. I rode atop the magnificent dildo float wearing black underwear, torn black hose, and S&M pumps.

The crowd split like the red sea as I rushed in like Pharaoh's Chariot chasing the slaves in Egypt. Through the audience of mostly hippies and some ladies who regularly attended the park's band shell every Sunday for the usual free classical concert, my slave boys pulled me toward the stage. The impact and sight of me, riding that gigantic dildo while whipping my slaves into submission, caused a few little old ladies to faint. Hands down I became the undisputed winner and was crowned queen of the prom, adding another step in my climb to fame, without fortune.

Along with the raves and fanfare, there were bruises on the road to stardom. After the show was over, while I was changing back into my overalls and flannel shirt in the park restroom, I watched Viva, now five—a mini diva in training—playing with my crown in the mirror. As she put it on her head, she proclaimed, "Mommy look, now I'm a queen too!"

When I came outside, I found that all my boys had disappeared, gone off to celebrate with new fans or tricks. As the fog rolled over the Haight, I walked home alone, pushing Viva in the dildo shopping cart. There was no way I was going to leave that valuable prop in the park. This was the price I paid for being a star in the Gay Counter Culture. No Backdoor Johnnies waiting to whisk me away in a limo or take me to fancy dinners at Sardis. I got to go home alone, schlepping the kid and props. It was my night to cook at the casa. It kept me humble.

Leather Queen at Roll Over Alice, Golden Gate Park, 1974
Roommate/slaves— Top row, left to right: Jimmy Evans, Mark America,
Martin, bottom row: David Venice, Me, and Michael McCarthy.

28

Mom-E-Quee-Rest

Outside of my father's reaction to Viva's mixed race, it never seemed to be an issue in my world. Viva was a gorgeous girl, the color of a good summer tan, and by the time she began school at age five I had let her curly hair grow long and wild. She looked like a tiny Chaka Khan, especially at parties when I let her wear my bright red lipstick.

At least once a week, I performed the same ritual with Viva after school. I'd sit on the stoop outside of Clayton Street, with Viva sitting between my legs on the step below me. Like a good hippy mom, I'd pour a few drops of Rosemary oil on my hair brush and begin to drag it through Viva's wild, wavy mop of knotted hair. This ritual of brushing the tangles out was not as much fun as dancing with a snake on her pretty head, but it had to be done. As the brush hit the first big clump, Viva whimpered.

"Am I hurting you honey?" I asked.

"No, Mommy, but I don't like rosemary oil. It smells funny," she answered.

"But sweetheart, rosemary oil is good; it makes your hair silky and shiny."

She raised the whimper a few decibels:

"Please, Mommy, the girls on the bus laugh at me. Can't you use Vaseline, like Lisa's mommy?"

"What girls?" I asked.

"The black ones, Mommy, they don't like me."

Until that moment I didn't have a clue about what my daughter was experiencing being of mixed races—what it was like for her to be a light skinned Afro-American with long wavy hair, free of kink. Like any mother, it hurt me to think of my little girl feeling any kind of pain, especially the pain of rejection.

"Oh honey, those girls are just jealous because you have pretty hair. Don't worry, I won't use rosemary oil anymore."

I suddenly was filled with guilt for not being more aware that my bright shining girl, the joy of my life, was having trouble in her first-grade class. I was living under the delusion that I was in touch with her every need. I assumed that she was content as long as she got to pal around with Mommy, and that the fact that she had few age-appropriate kids to play with didn't matter. I knew kids from straight families had normal playdates, but she had her drag-queen aunties to play dress-up with and teach her how to dance and sing. And I educated her in the arts—took her to plays, movies, concerts, and even the ballet. Before she was old enough to take classes herself, she got to sit in the back of all my tap and flamenco classes, and learned by observation. She could recite every line to every play I ever did from watching endless rehearsals and knew the lines better then the players themselves. I thought all that added up to being a good mother.

From infancy, I took Viva to the movies and she would sleep on my lap unless the volume jumped up suddenly, and then all I'd have to do was stick my boob in her mouth and she'd fall right back to sleep. It got more complicated seeing certain films as she got older. Viva often reminds me of the trauma I caused by taking her to see Brian Du Palma's horror classic, *Carrie,* when she was only four. She was so terrified that she kept hiding under her chair and I kept saying, "Get up off of that dirty sticky floor. You'll ruin your pretty dress." To this day, Viva can't watch a scary movie.

Unlike my mother, who cried over a burnt casserole, I never let Viva see me cry. I thought it was important to be strong. I buried my need for a man and father for her under the glitter and gaiety. Little did I know that I was teaching her to hide her deeper feelings from me too. I was trying to be the mother I wished I had had. In my defense, many of her influences were bright and helped her creative spirit soar. There was ample love and affection, but just not a whole lot of conscious child care. I was too busy trying to raise myself in my new family of arrested-developed adult children. As Joni Mitchell so eloquently reminded me every time I played the album *Blue*, I was still a "child with a child, pretending."

Mamma and Baby Diva going out on the town, 1974, Clayton Street

Viva with Uncle Tommy

Viva doing math homework

29

Sister Hags

I wasn't the only single mom living in a household of mostly gay men. Amber Waves, Esmeralda, Beaver Bauer, and Lenore were also hippy moms, and we shared a common bond. Beaver Bauer, a core member of the Angels of Light, was a luminous performer as well as a brilliant art director and costume designer. Beaver had a little boy name Sham, who was close to Viva's age. My earliest off-stage memory of Beaver brings to mind The Little Dutch Boy. Her short, bobbed, pretty-blonde head was always bent over a sewing machine, and on stage, her wholesome beauty was often hidden under gigantic costumes or pounds of makeup and glitter. My friendship with her grew gradually when we eventually got to work together in 1976, when I was invited to perform with the Angels in *Mind Kamp Kabaret* in 1976.

The *dishmongers* among the Angels called Lenore "The Breeder" because she had not one, but two daughters. She and her husband Tony had both been with the Living Theatre in New York. But Tony had left her and joined the

Angels. When Lenore discovered she was pregnant with a second child, she followed after her man. Ananda, her first-born, became Viva's first girlfriend.

Viva was four when I met Esmeralda, while she was still living in Mendocino with her two small children, Elo, five, and Lavender, three. Esmeralda, a petite gypsy with long, dark hair and American Indian features was a beauty. "Essie," as her friends called her, was recently divorced and had plans to move to the City to follow her dream of becoming a singer. As I sat at her homey kitchen table in a rustic, small, colorful house in the middle of a forest in Petaluma, she served me chamomile tea and confessed that she had been afraid to meet me. After seeing our mutual friend Jamian's film of my *Leather Queen* in the park, riding the big black dick chariot to stardom, Essie judged me. "I thought you were a real dominatrix. I said to Jamian, 'I don't ever want to meet that woman, she scares me.' You looked so evil whipping those boys." Once meeting me, she realized I was just a hippy mom like her, and what she saw was just good acting.

Amber Waves, a spacey redhead with piercing blue eyes, was one of the players from the Rollover Alice Company. Amber—originally Patty Pennington, an airline stewardess from Ohio before her reincarnation as Amber Waves—was a mystical showgirl, and had a young son named Sean. Sean's father was a junkie who left Amber early in their marriage. At the end of the *Rollover Alice* run, Amber approached me with a suggestion that we gather some of the best and brightest from *Rollover Alice* and Warped Floors and create a new show together. We enticed Joe Morocco, Candace, Eric, Scrumbly's roommate, and Scrumbly himself to be musical director, and got Martin to write lyrics and direct. Martin said, "Call your show *War Babies,* and I'll write numbers from every decade starting from WW2 till now."

It was a great concept for the show but not long into the planning, one by one, the War Babies began to drop like bombs on the shores of Normandy, leaving me and Amber the last two divas standing. Even though we still had the support of reliable Scrumbly and Martin, I was reluctant to take on the challenge of carrying the weight of a show with just Amber. In the short time I knew her, I could see that Amber was a handful, on and off stage, but she managed to persuade me to not abandon the project. Scrumbly and Martin had already written my first number for a '40s character, *The Wacky WAC from Hackensack"* and after the smash hit they created for me with *Tapping in a Varicose Vein*, I knew I had another showstopper.

Over the next few months Amber and I would drop our kids off at school and work on creating characters and numbers. I put on the producer hat and managed to attract a talented stage crew: my roommate Marshall and his lover, David Greene, both fantastic photographers, along with photographer Danny Nicoletta, who worked for Harvey Milk at Castro Camera. With the collected skills and talents of everyone, we ended up with a multimedia musical revue and called it *Broken Dishes*.

Danny and David, both budding filmmakers, co-directed a short 16 mm film of Amber and me playing juvenile delinquents, blowing smoke rings in the mirror of the Ladies Room inside the Castro Theatre while dreams of stardom shined in our eyes, ending with us both playing haggard housewives. The final frames of the film show Amber doing endless loads of laundry intercut with me smashing dirty dishes against my kitchen wall. It was quite a masterful piece of film that opened our show and made Amber and me look like major movie stars—or at least think we were.

With *Broken Dishes,* I had the opportunity to hone my skills as a producer, and Scrumbly brought in fantastic backup singers, A.C. Griffin and Tom Drain. Amber was dynamic and funny on stage, but very dysfunctional on the home front. I suppose it sounds like the pot calling the kettle black, but I was a lot less fragile than she and could handle a lot more responsibility. I found myself not only wearing the hats of writer, producer, costume designer and performer, but on some days I literally had to do Amber's laundry before I could get her out of the house to a rehearsal. Amber was so spacey that on one occasion she put her son to bed at a party and by the end of the evening she had forgotten she had a kid and went home without him.

I, the short zaftig brunette with a down-to-earth attitude, and Amber, the tall airy redhead with only one toe on the planet, were quickly forming the female counterparts to the Smother Brothers, *sans* guitars. We used our differences in physicality and personalities as fodder for our comedy, and our opening number was a sendup to the sister act played by Rosemary Clooney and Vera-Ellen in the movie *White Christmas*. Amber was unstoppable when it came to writing her songs and monologues; you could never get her to edit a word. I left my lyric writing to Martin, but wrote my own monologues, and we co-wrote our skits together.

Poster from Broken Dishes at the Palm Salon, 1976

30

What To Wear

I was thirty years old, and had been in San Francisco for only three years by the opening of *Broken Dishes* in the summer of 1976, the year of the U.S. bicentennial. I found an out-of-town venue for a test run before we opened in the city. I booked two consecutive weekends at the Mendocino Art Center. A few weeks before we were to open in Mendocino, we went up to The Albion Fair to do a little promo and attract the country audience for our upcoming show. Jamian invited us to ride up in his van and camp out overnight. My primary focus was on putting the show promo together, packing costumes, wigs and props, and I made the mistake of leaving the practical camping stuff to Amber. Amber and I were the queens of camp, but she, I soon learned, knew nothing about outdoor camping. Only when we began to unpack our show drag did I learn that Amber forgot the food and cooking aids. She hadn't even packed a can opener. If it weren't for the generous hippies we met, our children would have gone hungry that weekend.

One of those generous hippies was Lulu, a young talented dancer from Chicago who lived at Orr Hot Springs in Ukiah. Lulu was a rare breed of openly gay boy in the midst of a very straight rural community. He had a reputation for being a fantastic tap and belly dancer and was beloved by his very straight hippy neighbors. He was at the fair to belly dance. All dressed in our finery, with Lulu in his girly bellydance outfit clinking and clanking along the dusty dirt road to the stage, we were stopped dead in our tracks. A rowdy pack of Hells Angels pulled their motorcycles up and blocked our way. They singled out Lulu at the head of our procession. The leader of their pack yelled in his face, "Hey you, hey you, are you one of those fags we heard about, up here from San Francisco."

We were well aware of the Hells Angels' reputation at free concerts, so naturally we were terrified. Lulu looked the bully dead in the eye and with both hands on his hips and in the queeniest voice, said, "Why? What are you going to do to me if I tell you? Fuck me or kill me?"

His delivery was so funny that their leader cracked up and the whole gang followed his laughing like thugs in a Mafia movie. With the Hells Angels laughing their asses off, they gave us a motor escort all the way to the stage and that day the Hells Angels were Lulu's loudest fans. I saw a magician in Lulu, and I was determined to get him to move to San Francisco to work in our show. A few months later he did just that, and became our third backup boy.

Two weeks after the fair, the Mendocino opening of *Broken Dishes* did not go off without a hitch. Some of the conservative contributors to the Mendocino Art Center heard about the racy performers from San Francisco and they came out to scrutinize our dress rehearsal. A few members of the board of directors tiptoed into the back of the theatre just as Amber and I were doing "Beauty Secrets," our opening number. When I threw my arms up in the air, the uninvited guests caught me having a wardrobe malfunction. Both my boobs flung out of the corset that had yet to have the straps sewed on. If that wasn't bad enough, Amber was flashing her natural red pubes because she forgot to put her panties on under her corset. That's all these stuffed-shirts needed to see to send them running to complain to the artistic director. They demanded that the show be shut down before it even opened, due to indecency.

Back in our hotel room, as little Sean ran circles around his mom, Amber sat in a full lotus, wringing her hands and weeping, asking the Universe, "Why are they persecuting me for my spiritual work?" She kept casting tarot cards, and chanting Hail Marys. As she searched the tarot for an answer, I sprang into action. I left the hotel with Viva and we walked all over town trying to find some local liberals to become our allies. At a coffee house I met a gay man who had strong connections in the community and he helped me gather up some other people who offered support. They put counter pressure on the director of the Art Center. The word spread quickly around town that censorship was afoot and the stuffy board of directors caved. The following night *Broken Dishes* was allowed to open as planned.

There were technical problems as well. The theatre had been built with a beautiful skylight in the center over the house seats, and in the summertime it was difficult to make the house dark enough to show the film that opened the show. The tickets were sold for an 8 p.m. curtain, but we had to postpone the show until 9 p.m.

The word-of-mouth controversy gave us more publicity than we could ever have paid for. The doors opened to an oversold house that had been gathering outside for over an hour. More than halfway through the show, all was going very well when an unexpected flash thunderstorm arrived with a bang. With the first crack of thunder, we lost all electrical power in the middle of Amber's best song, "The

Rhinestone Blues." Amber and Scrumbly, troupers that they were, didn't miss a beat, and they kept playing and singing in the dark. Just as Amber sang the lyric, "So light my cigarette," as if God himself had written the scene, on cue, the entire theatre lit up from the lightening flashing overhead. Throughout the remainder of the song, the lightening kept the show illuminated, giving our stagehands time to find candles and flashlights so we could continue the show. That night we won the hearts of our new fans, and even of some enemies. I took credit for my practical knowledge, and Amber thanked magic and witchcraft, but it was clear to me that *Broken Dishes* had been born by Grace.

Poster from Broken Dishes Mabuhay Gardens, 1977

31

I Love Fags

I'm not going to tell you about every boy I ever loved or slept with because if I do you'll only think I'm bragging. Like designer labels, Fag Hag, Bitch, Witch and Whore were terms I wore proudly. Martin Worman taught me that the word *fag* meant *twig*. Fags were the boys used as kindling on the pilings used to torch witches. The fags were sacrificed merely for associating with or loving the women who were persecuted for showing their power and their spiritual gifts. Martin explained that fags and hags made one hell of a hot bonfire.

I must have been one of those witches in a previous life, and now I was being reunited with my fellow victims from the past. It was one way to explain my attraction to gay men. My gay lovers were not monogamous and never promised me happy-ever-afters. We were more like polygamists in a Mormon cult (sort of), except that in the gay counterculture, we did it with style. My housemate Marshall loved to tease me about my trysts with gay men. He said I had "fag attraction" and no one could understand why so many queers always ended up in my bed. Neither could I.

I felt adored like Ava Garner in the film *One Touch of Venus*, who turned from stone to flesh and came down from a pedestal to experience the love of her suitor. I was not like some fag hags, making a sport of getting a gay boy to bed. Most of my lovers evolved naturally out of friendships. I was always surprised when an innocent love crossed the line. I had many intimate affairs; some were one night stands and others lasted longer, but when the lover label faded away—or, as in some cases, was ripped off like a hot Brazilian bikini wax—these relationships always reverted back to lasting friendships.

Many years after my party days ended, while working on my sobriety, I wrote a list of everyone I ever slept with. I came up with 154 names. That number did not include everyone. There were some I didn't remember. One day I bumped into a chubby chaser trying to pick up women at an Overeaters Anonymous meeting and he approached me at the coffee table at the back of the meeting hall.

"Hi, my name is Billy; didn't we have sex at Harbin Hot Springs in 1974?" he asked.

Caught off guard, I just stared at him with a quizzical look on my face.

"Don't you remember?" he said, "I was the guy who *Watsued* you."

"I remember Watsu; it's Shiatsu underwater," I said and walked away.

The words *sex* and *love* were never used in connection with addiction in the '70s. But today I could admit that I probably fit the criteria for your classic sex and love addict according to the twelve-step model. Sex was never my goal; it was love I ached for.

Innocence and denial was bliss in my big incestuous family where we swapped lovers and rolls more frequently than we changed our drag. Loving unavailable men kept me safe from vulnerability and painful rejection from straight men. I had so many friends, fans and suitors in my delirious youth that I never worried about what tomorrow would bring. I even felt superior to the typical conventional woman who had to rely on one man to meet all her needs when I always had a dozen or more.

My friends and lovers often served as my gay husbands. They mentored me, fed me, dressed me, cared for me and my daughter, and made love to me even when I felt less than worthy. They helped me laugh off my deep loneliness, and when I couldn't, offered me a shoulder to cry on.

Bobby Star &
Pristine Condition
*Photo by
Michael Zagaris*

Martin Worman &
Scrumbly Koldwyn
Photo by Dan Nicoletta

32

John

I met John McGuire in 1973 and his partner Tim McKenna while on a vacation in Mazatlán, Mexico, right after my San Francisco debut of *Cinderella*. John was short and tan with piercing green eyes, and Tim, his opposite, was long, lean and blond. I literally fell into his arms on the balcony of my motel while running from my crazy traveling companion, Charles Isis. Charles was a bit player I had met among the extras who hung out at the Ranch during *Cinderella* rehearsals earlier that year. Joe Morocco had invited me to join him and all his housemates on a trip to Mexico. I arranged to have my friend Karen and her little boy stay with Viva for a week at my place in Venice, but when the time came to go, everyone in San Francisco had bowed out except for Charles, and I ended up alone with him on a thirty-hour bus ride down to Mazatlán. The bus ride was only made worse by the fact that, after a few hours in, I realized I had caught scabies during a casual three-way back home in Venice with Dorsey and his fiancée, Karen Dunaway.

I should have known the trip was doomed when my new theater friends cancelled and left me with only Charles, who I barely knew. Charles showed no sympathy as itchy colonies of microscopic scabies were multiplying under my skin faster than fruit flies on a ripe banana.

By the time we arrived in Mazatlán it was Mardi Gras, and the raucous celebrations included gunshots and fireworks. This did not make for a soothing vacation for a tourist with a full-blown case of scabies. I sought help at a Mexican pharmacy, but due to the language barrier, I came away with the wrong remedy, Scabison Emulsion, a lotion intended for lice on livestock. I slathered it liberally all over my body, and as soon as the burning began I jumped into a shower so hot as to be almost fatal. This only caused my pores to open more and the poison began to eat through all seven layers of my skin. After switching to the cold water to slow the burn, I emerged from the bath in my towel crying only to find my traveling buddy Charles up to no good.

Charles was on the bed with two underage Mexican boys. One boy was nodding out while Charles was tying a tourniquet around the arm of the other boy, about to shoot him up with heroin. Horrified, I screamed and ran from the scene—right into the arms of John, who was just coming back from the beach. John took me into his room and he and Tim calmed me down. After awhile we went back to my room to retrieve my clothes. Charles and the boys were out so I packed my things and put them in their room. John and Tim brought me back to the pharmacy to get the antidote for Scabison Emulsion and then invited me to travel back to the U.S. with them the next day.

A month later, when I found my apartment on Clayton Street, I learned that John and Tim were my neighbors, living down the block on the corner of Waller Street. John and I were both short Italian Americans who loved to cook and dance. At that time, John was a chef at an upscale vegetarian restaurant on Polk Street and taught me how to make the best tofu burgers I've ever had. I still make them to this day. It was easy to love John, whose compact muscular body reminded me of the bad boys I knew in high school. Our bond was as thick as his chunky marinara sauce, and like a big brother, John was always protective of me and Viva. He fancied the idea of us being a family.

I never knew if John's partner Tim knew that John, on occasion, would sleep with me, but if Tim knew, he never expressed any jealousy. Tim was Sylvester's manager before Sylvester became world renowned for his disco hits. The first time I saw Sylvester on stage at The City, a popular gay cabaret and disco, he was making magic by singing a sultry blues that would give Billie and Ella a run for their money. Sylvester was wearing a shimmering wing-sleeved sequined blue dress, and the moody stage lights bouncing off the dress filled the room with sparkles like a disco ball—a preview of the days that would follow when Sylvester's music filled the discos for decades.

As Tim was working hard to build Sylvester's fame and fortune, John and I got to sit front-row, center at every one of Sylvester's shows. After a fun night of blues, and rocking gospel with Sylvester wailing at The City, Sylvester would often invite us back to his home for a small after-hours gathering. I loved those late nights when Sly would take off his wig and put on a comfortable robe, and then we would all pile on his bed where he held court and shared joints and stories. To be in the company of a genius diva stripped down to a warm, earthy goddess at home was a privilege. Like a gracious queen, Sylvester entertained her subjects as she held court in bed. I took notes.

Another thing that John and I had in common was our love of gospel music, and on Sundays John would take Viva and me to the Glide Memorial Church or to special Bay Area Gospel Choirs competitions. John and I would get down like two old church ladies, stomping and shouting and falling out with the best of them.

One afternoon John came by and told me to get dressed because he was taking me to a party to meet his yoga teacher. We arrived at a deluxe home in the upscale Berkeley Hills. I had no idea of what to expect. I had dressed in my best vintage Dorothy Lamour '40s print sarong and slipped into my highest heeled platforms and put on my signature bright red lips.

When I entered the ritzy foyer with my heels clanking on the tile floor, a pious group of barefooted yoga students in white pajamas, who were all meditating in the living room, opened their eyes and turned toward me in unison. From their seated lotus positions, their expressions changed from bliss to disdain. But before they could run me off for the rude disturbance, I was greeted by a friendly Indian man with a long salt-and-pepper beard, dressed in traditional Indian garb. As he entered the foyer, John introduced me to his yoga master, Swami Shiva Lignum. John explained later that the name meant God's Penis in Hindi. Swami Ji took one look at me and embraced me like an old friend, then whisked me away into the kitchen where he was preparing an Indian feast for his students. That day he taught me and John how to make chapati and kept the other humble students in the front room turning green with envy when they saw that, without ever removing my shoes or doing one single posture, I had been made Swami Ji's teacher's pet. After that initial meeting, I became Swami Shiva Lignum's disciple and joined John in his yoga practice.

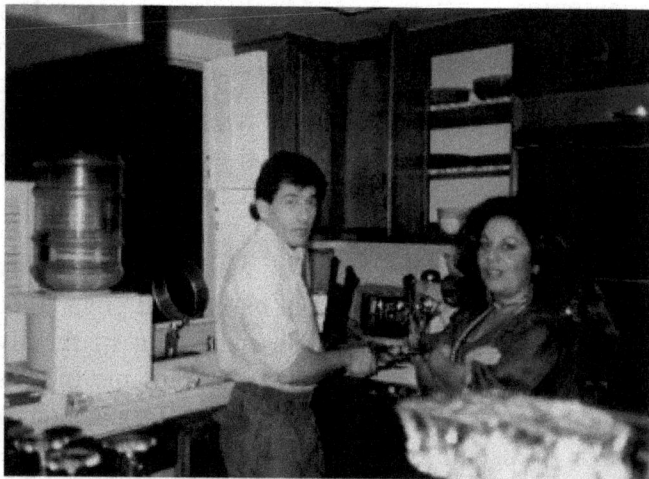

Cooking with John McGuire

33

Lendon

I first met Lendon when he bounded up my steps one afternoon looking for my roommate Jimmy and his lover Gil. Lendon was a Cockette, but he had moved to L.A. just before I arrived on the scene in San Francisco. After a dinner with our roommates, Lendon invited me to join him and the boys at the Stud where every night gorgeous men filled the amyl nitrite-scented dance floor. At the bar, Lendon greeted a few old friends, but for the most part remained close to my side and danced with me the whole night. After we got back home, Jimmy and Gil gave Lendon a blanket and directed him toward the couch, and they went to bed. I don't recall if I invited him or if he invited himself, but somehow Lendon was sharing my bed. Even after all the attention he had paid to me, it never occurred to me that this magnificent African prince with his regal ebony features and short dreadlocks would ever in a million years want to sleep with me. Sex was instant, easy and natural with him, and Lendon fit me like my favorite pair of cozy flannel pajamas. His dark skin radiated so much warmth that I had to turn off the heater in my room that night.

The next day, Lendon met Viva. In the two years we had lived in San Francisco, Viva rarely saw her dad, and there was a shortage of African American male role models in our immediate community. When she saw Lendon she practically leapt into his arms. Lendon came from warm southern roots and embraced my child, and they bonded instantly, just as we had. Lendon spent the remainder of his week with us. To the outside world we looked like the perfect bi-racial family everywhere we went. When he had to go back to L.A., he invited me to come visit him as soon as I could get away.

My perfect family fantasy picked up where it left off during the weekend Viva and I stayed with Lendon at his little guest house in the San Fernando Valley. After he played daddy all day and put Viva to bed, we sat in the swing under the lemon trees in the back yard on an unusually warm winter night. That night, Lendon held me in his arms and read poetry to me. He chose a poem from Walt Whitman.

Are you the new person drawn toward me?
To begin with, take warning—I am surely far different from what you
suppose;
Do you suppose you will find in me your ideal?
Do you think it so easy to have me become your lover?
Do you think the friendship of me would be unalloy'd
satisfaction?
Do you think I am trusty and faithful?
Do you see no further than this façade—this smooth and tolerant
manner of me?
Do you suppose yourself advancing on real ground toward
a real heroic man?

*Have you no thought, O dreamer, that it may be all Maya,
illusion?*

That night we spooned in bed, and I ignored the warning
in the poem he read. I drifted off to sleep to the tones of
Roberta Flack singing "Killing Me Softly." This was not
the first affair that sent my mind wandering down the aisle,
thinking, "Could this bi-boy be the one, the one who will
be mine forever?" But it wasn't long before reality would
bitch-slap me upside the head.

The next night at the Pink Elephant, a Venice gay bar, I
introduced Lendon to David Greene, the filmmaker who
worked on *Broken Dishes*. By the end of the night, it
became clear that Lendon and David were totally smitten
with one another. After closing, David and Lendon asked
for my blessing before they went off to consummate their
newfound love for one another.

"Of course, haven't I been taught to share? Have a good
time."

I left the bar wearing my comedy mask, but once alone
again, the tragedy hit me. On the drive back home, deep
sadness and dark despair gripped my heart.

As I pulled unto the I-10 freeway to head back to pick
up Viva from the sitter, my pain once again was
highlighted by that damn song "Killing Me Softly," playing
on my car radio. Roberta's sweet words turned to vinegar
but I refused the sour in the pit of my stomach and choked
back the tears. I floored my little VW Bug to 70 miles an
hour and let Ms. Flack say it for me, "and then he looked
right through me as if I wasn't there. He was killing me
softly with his song…"

I convinced myself that losing a man to a man was
easier than losing him to another woman. Shattered
romance is never easy, but this loss came cloaked in
adoration. The consolation prize is that both Lendon and

David are still together today, and still my good friends after all these years.

Me and Lendon,
Venice 1977
Photo by David Greene

Me and Gregory Angel
Photo by Dan Nicoletta

34

WOPS

Had he not been a queer, Tommy Pace would have made the perfect husband—the Italian/American husband my parents prayed I'd find. Although he was only half Italian, we shared a mutual love for all things Italian, including the insulting slang words like *dago* or *WOP* that labeled Italian immigrants without papers when they arrived at Ellis Island. This politically incorrect lingo was the language of our love.

"Girl, you are just a faggot trapped in a woman's body, and I'm your dyke trapped in a faggot's body." Tommy whispered in my ear as we lay on his tiny bed in a cluttered basement of the small house on Wilmot Street near the Fillmore. I met Tommy while out shopping with Marshall at the Purple Heart Thrift Store on Mission Street. Tommy had long, dark hair and he kept flipping it about like a girl in a shampoo commercial. He was cute enough, but I was so consumed by my own divahood that I didn't register his gorgeous pouty lips, chiseled high cheekbones and chestnut-brown eyes until months later. Amber already knew Tommy from the *Rollover Alice* production, and when we were re-mounting *Broken Dishes* for our first City run, she asked me if we could find a small part for Tommy in the show. Even though we already had too many backup boys, Amber convinced me to give him a little walk-on where he got to usher her boozy starlet character off the stage with a funny line.

One night, Tommy and I grabbed a bite at Little Joe's, a popular hole-in-the-wall off of Columbus Ave. in North Beach. The restaurant had only a few tables covered in red-and-white-checkered tablecloths and a long counter where you could watch the cooks stir up hot Italian dishes before your eyes. Garlic filled your nostrils as the pots and pans flew through the air. As the cooks whipped up their bestseller, ziti with broccoli, garlic and olive oil, we waited for a spot to open at the counter. Tommy asked what I thought of him when we first met. I couldn't remember. "I thought you were fat and spacey," I said. He wasn't at all fat, but I knew he was vain and a good verbal love slap was like foreplay. After that night, Tommy followed me around like a puppy.

Tommy was a macho "Guido" trapped inside a flaming queen, and he played both roles to the hilt. With food and words, we roleplayed the WOP *Honeymooners* version of Ralph and Alice. Over a steaming bowl of rigatoni, he tenderly whispered sweet nothings like: "pass the cheese you dumb dago bitch," and "just you wait, one of these days, Mary, one of these days, I'm gonna slip you the salami."

I laughed, "You think you have the meat balls for that Renaldo?"

That night, lying in his bed after a heavy carb loading and a Quaalude chaser, I let Tommy slip me the salami and I allowed the man in me to fall deeply for the woman in him.

Tommy's humor made me weak in the knees and he could literally hypnotize me by lightly tickling my arms with his long, sharp fingernails. The first time Tommy tickled my arms, I flashed back to the time when my dad tickled my arms the same way, when I had horrible cramps from my period. Tommy had my dad's deep, dark eyes, but Daddy never had Tommy's sharp nails.

Over the years, Tommy and I would fall in and out of love, but never out of friendship. Our most intimate moments involved food. Like when he ordered Ziti Arabiatta to cheer me up after I aborted an unplanned pregnancy caused not by him, but by his friend and co-star, John Sokoloff, in The Gay Men's Theatre Collective.

We had just left the clinic and I was feeling relief. I knew the last thing I needed was another child with an unavailable father. Tommy had been very sweet to me; then, as soon as we ordered, he turned on me. "Girl, what were you thinking when you let the queen fuck you without a rubber?" he said.

"I don't know." I sulked. "It happened after a twilight matinee of *Looking for Mr. Goodbar*. The movie made me so anxious that John invited me back to his place for drinks to calm my nerves. Well, you know what a lightweight I am. When I admired the upside-down crucifix over his wrought-iron bedpost, I ended up on the bed with my heels over my head and him telling me how good I tasted."

"You couldn't stop there, could you? But no, you just had to have the salami. What were you thinking?" he said. Then the next second he was soothing and worrying over me. "Never mind, eat your meatballs. You need the iron. Are you still cramping?"

Pasta was the glue that held us together, and over many a meal, we downed starch blockers, a class of diet wonder-drugs that promised freedom to eat as much pasta as you liked without gaining a pound. We ate ourselves into oblivion knowing that starch-blocker claims were too good to be true. After those meals, Tommy would walk behind me cursing as he had to push me up the steep hill on Clayton Street to get me home. Whenever we were out late, he'd pick Viva up from Mrs. Robinson, the sitter, and carry her up to bed. One night I overheard him as he tucked her in.

"Okay, my queen, now get your butt back to sleep, you know, girl, you need your booty rest."

"Mommy says you need to give your booty a rest because you're the evil queen, I'm still a princess, 'cause I'm only five."

By 1977 we were like two old farts together. Tommy and I needed roleplaying to spark our love life. His favorite turn-on was me wearing an ugly flannel nightgown that he bought for me from the Hadassah Thrift Store. He said it made me look like the Polynesian Princess in *South Pacific*. On nights when I over-ate and felt too bloated for sex, he made me put on the unflattering flannel nightgown, and it was just enough to send him into a medley. This was Tommy's way to get me in the mood. He started singing "Happy Talk," and by the time he began hitting the high falsetto notes of "Bali High," he had me. It's amazing that we could have sex at all, since I could never stop laughing. There were days and nights when Tommy made me laugh so hard that I'd wake up the next day with pain in my abdomen as if I had done too many sit-ups at the gym.

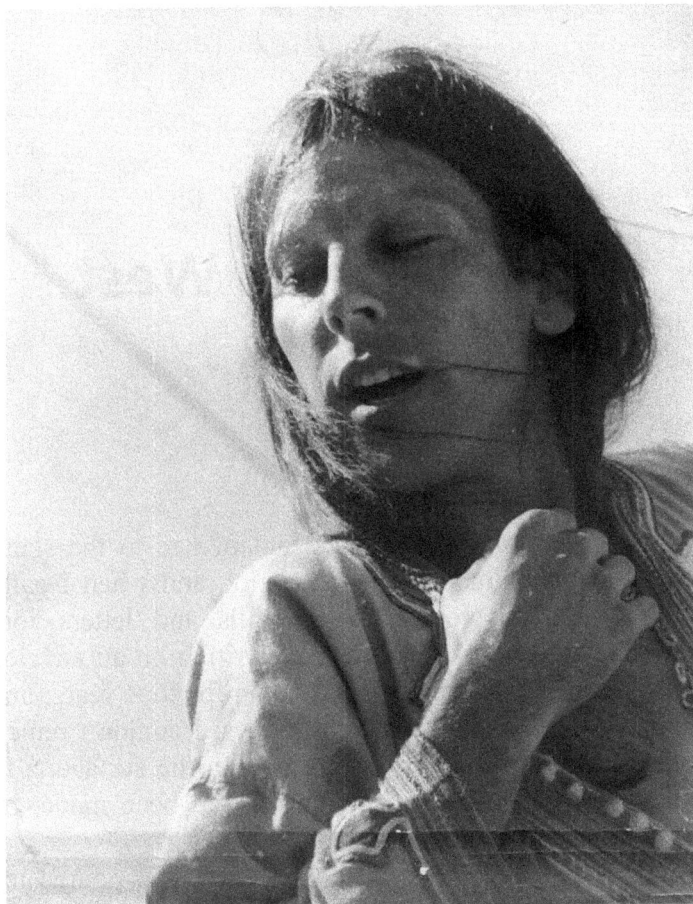

Tommy Pace

35

East Meets West

One morning I crawled out of bed to the sound of
mail falling through the slot, and when I gathered
the envelopes—mostly bills and letters for my
roommates—I saw familiar handwriting on an envelope—
my mother's. I hadn't visited home for four years, and we
talked only on holidays or birthdays; I couldn't remember
the last time she'd written to me. On the surface, a peace
treaty between me and my father had been made, but in
reality, a cold war still waged.

I dropped the bills on the kitchen table, poured myself
some coffee and went back to bed to open the letter. I
needed caffeine for that. It was unusually quiet for a
Saturday morning, Viva had a sleep-over with Lisa and
Mrs. Robinson took the girls to the park early. As I tore
open Mom's letter I read,

Dear Dee, I hope you are doing good. Your dad had a
quadruple bypass but don't worry he's doing really good
now. Everything's back to normal. I would-a told ya sooner

*but he didn't want you to know. That's your father, what
can I say? Now that he's better he wants to take a vacation.
We are going to Tahoe to see Aunt Mary and her family.
All but Ginny cause she can't leave her job or her husband
for long. Since we are out that far, we thought we'd visit
you in San Francisco too. Your brother is so excited to
come back to California and I can't wait to see Viva and
your beautiful home. Your father can't wait too. We'll take
the bus from Lake Tahoe and maybe you can pick us up at
the Greyhound station since we don't know our way
around. I'll call you from Aunt Mary's when we get there
next week with the details. Okay.*

Love Mommy.

Their timing could not have been worse. Later that day,
at the market, I put several brands of disinfectants into my
shopping cart although I knew I could never clean my
house enough to meet my mother's standards, let alone hide
anyone's race or sexual orientation. I could not imagine my
dad, a Nixon-loving Republican, conversing with my
commie-loving, drag-queen roomies. Short of boarding off
Debbie's room, I was stumped for any ideas on how not to
make my parents' visit an entrance into *The Twilight Zone*.
At dinner, I dropped the bomb about my folks landing on
us, and hoped that my roommates might consider toning
down the drag to help make my family feel at ease.

Marshall said, "Girl, what do they think of Jews? I can
be your beard if you like."

"Yeah, and I'll dress up as Bessie the maid and call you
Missy Deluxe," Jerry added. I knew that the best I could do
was pray that everyone would be out when I brought my
parents to see where I lived. The only practical help I got
was from Tommy, who offered to find them a bed and
breakfast in Little Italy.

The day they arrived was a typical cold, foggy summer
day. I dressed Viva in her prettiest dress and off we went in

my VW bug to meet the Greyhound at the downtown station. As my parents stepped off the bus, I saw that my dad was still as handsome as ever, but he looked tired. Mom, ten pounds heavier, was her usual jumble of nerves and my brother, Richie, was fourteen and sporting a shadow of a mustache.

Viva had just turned six, and she hadn't seen them except in photographs. She was excited to meet them. Mom made a big fuss over her while Dad hugged me for what felt like a very long time.

Then he bent down to hug Viva. "Look at you, what a pretty girl you have grown into."

We made small talk as their bags were being unloaded from the storage under the bus, and then I helped them carry their luggage to my car. The streets were lined with winos panhandling in front of the station, and I became anxious about their first impression of the City. Mom clutched her purse and began to complain about the weather. I had warned her about the cold summer days, but she had only brought a light sweater.

I tightly squeezed their luggage in the small trunk of my car and Dad took the front seat, while Mom and Richie, with Viva on his lap, sat in the back.

"I hope we don't have to drive on any highways in this contraption," Mom said. "Ya know, Dee, I didn't tell ya the whole story about your father because we didn't want ya to worry. Ya shoulda seen how he suffered, and he never even complained."

"How could he? You take the cake in the complaint department," Richie said.

Dad was very quiet and didn't even try to stifle Mom like he used to. He let her ramble on while he silently soaked in the sights of the charming streetcars as we drove past them. But when Mom started to bring to light the gory details of Dad's surgery, he interrupted her.

"Gloria, *stata chit*, it was nothing, I'm just like new, even better than before, the doctor says."

"I just want Dee to know in case something could happen. Ya never know. I hope you have a good Doctor, just in case," she asked.

Then Mom turned her attention to Viva. "I can't believe you're such a big girl already. I hope the new dresses I bought you at Sears still fit. I hope you like them."

Viva, on her best behavior, said, "Grandma, I'm sure I'll like them as long as you taste good." My brother cracked up.

"Honey, you mean have good taste," I said.

"Isn't that cute, John, the way she expresses herself," my mother said.

"Yeah she's smart just like her mother," Dad said.

I couldn't help noticing my dad's effort to make me feel good, and I wanted to melt, but still felt uneasy thinking about their reaction once they saw where I lived and met my roommates.

As I looked for a place to park on my block an awkward pause filled the air when my parents noticed a bearded man in a '40s print dress and high heels stumbling down the hill. I didn't bother to mention that he was one of my roommates. I got lucky and found a spot almost in front of my building. When Mom stepped out of the car, she clutched her bag as though at any second she expected a mugger to lunge at her. I quickly herded the family into my hallway, and the minute my mother saw the long flight of steps she started in with the complaining. "This can't be good for your father's heart; it's dangerous if he has to climb too many hills or stairs."

"Mom, it's going to be fine. Dad can take his time. My friend Tommy found you a beautiful Bed and Breakfast in North Beach. It's on a street that's not too steep and you'll have a room on the first floor. Tommy's folks always stay there when they come to visit. He's coming by to take us all there in a big car.

Viva added, "You guys are going to love my Uncle Tommy, he's not my real uncle like you, Uncle Richie, but I know him better."

"This Tommy, is he your boyfriend, Dee?" Mom asked as she paused on the steps.

"No Ma; we're just good friends."

When we reached the landing, Jerry popped out of his room to greet us, "Hey, guys, how ya doing?"

I made the introductions and Jerry, looking quite toned down from his daily flamboyance, extended his hand to my dad and in a deep, masculine voice, a full octave lower than his usual range, said, "Nice to finally meet the folks, I've heard so much about you." Then he turned to my brother, "This could not possibly be your baby brother Richie?"

"Yeah, they never let me forget it."

At that point Jerry invited my folks to tea and coffee and a snack that he had prepared for us.

"Well this is something. What do they call this, a railroad flat? Reminds me of the place we lived in when we was first married, John," Mom said.

We passed by the closed bedroom doors, and I showed them my room and Viva's room decorated all in pink for the princess of the manor. My folks seemed most impressed with our artsy kitchen and the giant vegetable mural on the wall. Then we adjourned to the living room where my folks sat on the rattan sectional under the painted palm tree murals.

"This is so fuckin' cool, it's like you guys live in a museum. I want to stay here," Richie said.

Viva said, "You can take my princess castle and I can sleep with Mommy."

Dad moved forward in his seat and gave Richie a stern look, "Rich, remember I told you, we don't want to put your sister out. Your mother and I are renting a hotel for us."

I was leery of Jerry's gracious hosting manners as he poured the coffee, acting like the house servant, a brand new role for him. My folks were eating it up.

"Isn't that something, the way the men are so helpful here in California?" Mom said. Then she turned to Jerry, "I could use a maid like you back home."

I was thinking, oh no, she practically called him Aunt Jemima. I sat there on pins and needles thinking that Jerry might go off at any moment. I had seen him on more than one occasion turn into a very vocal angry Negro over less. He smiled and let the comment go by.

As everyone was enjoying their sandwiches, I sat there shredding my napkin unconsciously. I was pretty certain that my father had never broken bread with a black man before, so I was surprised when Dad started to interview Jerry as if he were one of my suitors, "So, Dee tells us you're a singer. Can you make a living from that singing thing you do?"

"I'm doing all right," Jerry answered. "But not as well as your *paisan*, Mr. Frank Sinatra, that's for sure." And then he sang out, "But I'm doing it my way."

Mom applauded. "That's really good. I'm sure if Frank ever heard ya sing, he'd give ya a chance, just like he did with Sammy Davis Jr."

"That would be wonderful, and do you have any connections to Mr. Sinatra?" he asked my mother.

"Well as a matter of fact, Jerry, I don't like to brag, but I had a third cousin who was a distant relation to Frank. Unfortunately, he got shot in a phone booth, but I bet if I could get Frank's number and mention my cousin's name, he'd be very nice to me, I'm sure."

As Jerry listened patiently, I was dumbfounded by my good luck, everyone was out and the most outrageous queen of all was on his best behavior, actually amusing and putting my parents at ease. Jerry excused himself to get ready for work and we sat in an awkward pause once again.

"Grandpa, can Uncle Richie stay in my room? He would fit just right in my bed," Viva asked.

"Yeah, Rich said, "Just like Goldielocks. Dad, how about it? If I stay with Dee and Viva, then you and mom can have that second honeymoon you've been talking about for years."

"That's enough, smart mouth," Mom snapped.

Dad muttered, "We'll think about it."

Just then Jerry swung back though the door, twirling like Loretta Young making an entrance in her '50s TV show, wearing a floor-length, fur-lined, gold lamé coat. At the top of his falsetto, Jerry squealed, "Girl, what do you think of my new coat? Sylvester gave it to me."

My mother gasped, "Where would you wear something like that?"

"For the stage, mom," I jumped in. "It's a costume for the stage."

"Yeah, Grandma, it's drag," Viva added. "Don't you know about drag? Everybody wears it, even me. Mommy says I'm a drag queen in training."

At that, Jerry kissed Viva on both cheeks, preparing his exit. "So nice meeting you folks," and then turned to me and planted a big sloppy kiss on my lips. "Gotta run, ta-ta," and he sailed out the door with his gold lamé trailing behind him.

As soon as he was gone, Mom caught her breath and asked, "Dee, tell me something, is Jerry, how do they call it, Gay?"

Richie made a limp wrist/raised pinkie finger gesture while singing out loud, "He does it his way!" I could see the wheels spinning in Mom's head as she tried to figure if Jerry was a fag, or if he was fucking me, or both.

Dad did not say a word. The silence was broken when Tommy yelled out from down the hall, "Honey I'm home."

He entered carrying a gigantic bouquet of roses and put them in my mother's lap. "Welcome to San Francisco," he said.

Viva excitedly made the introductions, "Hey everybody, meet my Uncle Tommy." In unison, my folks let out a sigh of relief.

As Tommy hugged Viva, I watched my mother lean over to Dad and I heard her whisper, "Thank God, he looks Italian."

During the two days that followed, Tommy accompanied me on every outing with my family. We had several meals in Chinatown and Little Italy, and took them to all the tourist spots: the cable car rides, Lombard Street, and Fisherman's Warf. Except for Mom's constant complaining, my family seemed content.

While we were enjoying a great seafood dinner on the Warf, and Mom was slurping down her favorite oysters on a half shell, Tommy out of nowhere asked, "Would you like to meet my parents? They live in San Jose, just an hour from here." I kicked Tommy under the table. "My dad would love you guys," Tommy said. "You know he's Italian, but Mom is Irish and always says she's Italian by injection."

My parents laughed.

The northern California countryside brought Dad back to pleasant memories of his childhood in Southern Italy. We picked fresh figs off trees that grew outside our bed and breakfast in Napa. I could see a real change had come over him. Perhaps it was his near fatal heart attack that softened him, but it was obvious that this visit was his way of making amends, and he was doing his best to accept me. For the first time in a very long time, I felt compassion for my dad. I sat down close to him on the grass under the tree.

"Hey Dad, once you retire you might want to think about moving out here. You won't have to shovel snow anymore," I said.

"Sounds good."

Mom seemed threatened by my father's new serenity. When Dad mentioned that it might be a good idea to retire in Northern California over dinner that night, she sulked and said," Yeah sure, just like that; you expect me to move away from our families? You're nuts!"

The next day I brought my family to the airport and as we waited for the check at the coffee shop, Richie and Viva hung out at the window watching the planes take off and land.

"You know, you should marry Tommy. He's a good man; his hair is too long, but I can tell he really loves your kid," Mom said.

"Mom, Tommy's not husband material, we are just good friends."

"But friends make the best husbands. He looks like a keeper to me."

"Mom, I really don't think marriage is in the cards for us."

Then my father chimed in, "You could do a lot worse. Tommy's a little *cappo fresca,* but a real nice boy. You're lucky that any guy would want you with a kid that's not his own, especially in your circumstances."

"I'm lucky?"

Mom defended their argument, "You can't fault your father for wanting to dance at his daughter's wedding?"

I took the last gulp of my coffee to wash down the anger building. "You were both so excited that Tommy wasn't black that you failed to notice that he's queer."

"What a ya gonna do, live in a flat with no carpets on the floor with a bunch of strangers for the rest of your life? Just don't come crying home to me if you end up alone without a pot to piss in," Dad said raising his voice.

"Have I ever asked you for a dime? While you were ignoring us for the last six years, those so-called strangers were my family," I yelled.

Then Mom turned on the water works, "Alright already, stop arguing. It's not good for your father's heart."

"Why not blame me for that too while you're at it?"

The boarding call for Newark came over the loudspeaker. The argument stopped abruptly when Richie and Viva came back to the table. I hugged Richie. Mom, who was still in tears, hugged Viva.

"Don't cry grandma, I'll come to visit soon."

Dad gave Viva a hug and kissed her on both cheeks and turned his back to me and started to walk toward the boarding ramp. Mom and Richie followed him, but unlike Dad, they kept looking back and waving until they were out of sight.

As we walked to the car, Viva said, "What's wrong Mommy, you look like sad grandma?"

"Nothing sweetie, goodbyes make me sad, that's all."

36

Feel Me Heal Me

Although I practiced Yoga religiously and read the popular spiritual books of the day like: *Autobiography of a Yogi, Seth Speaks, Be Here Now,* and *The Lazy Man's Guide to Enlightenment,* I was a reluctant seeker. I had worshipped at the Altar of the Trinity: Drugs, Sex, and Disco, but my only Higher Power at that time was theatre and performance.

Just when I needed it the most, an amazing healer came into my life—a long-haired, handsome Japanese Buddhist named Reuho Yamada. Born in an old Zen temple in Beppu, Japan, Reuho was the son of a devoted temple wife and the head priest of the temple, Choshoji. From age three, Reuho was dressed in formal Zen robes and accompanied his father on his service rounds. Throughout Reuho's education he studied English and learned Shiatsu from a Zen Shiatsu Master, which led him to the West and the Zen Center at Tassajara. Reuho decided that hippies had a lot to teach him and made a choice to expand his consciousness with mind-altering drugs. But when I first met Reuho, he was as pure as his Buddhist lineage name "Ungai Reuho Dai Osho" would suggest. "Out from a Cloud, the Dharma/Treasure of the Dragon-Great Teacher/Priest."

One of Lulu's friends, a pretty Jewish princess from the Bronx, Shirley Flowers, discovered Reuho. There were few straight boys to go around in San Francisco, and Shirley saw him first. She made it her mission to serve his mission, and made him her lover. I recall the first day she brought him to Clayton Street in 1976. Reuho had long, straight, jet-black hair and wore wire-rim glasses. He looked like an Asian John Lennon. Shirley paraded her exotic conquest up to our apartment and introduced us.

Before I knew it, Reuho left Shirley in the kitchen chatting with my roommates and we were on the floor in my bedroom where he began treating me to one of his miraculous shiatsu massages. He spent the next three hours placing the tips of his thumbs deep into my flesh at many critical pressure points. I had had massages before, but nothing like this. It was as if Reuho was a skilled psychic surgeon who used his thumbs like a knife. As he plunged deep within me and held each point, I could feel lifetimes of pain leave my body. At the end of this session he bowed and thanked me, and then Shirley entered the room and suggested how I might repay his kindness. Shirley knew I sold LSD on occasion to supplement my welfare checks, and she let me know that Reuho would appreciate getting high. Rumors were circulated that Reuho had been the Shiatsu practitioner to his Holiness the Dalai Lama, and Shirley, an ambitious woman, soon turned their lavish Pacific Heights apartment into the Temple of the Lotus Flowers where monks, punks, hippies and artists would gather to discuss principles of Zen and healing while Shirley collected donations to pay the rent.

It seemed that whenever I was at my lowest, Reuho would just appear at my door to give me one of his remarkable healings. The day after my family left town,

Reuho showed up at my door. I never needed to use the phone. I was in a heap under the covers with a severe migraine. The upset with my parents and the pressure of opening *Broken Dishes* for our second City run had gotten the best of me. Usually Reuho was silent in deep meditation while treating me, but on this day throughout the massage, Reuho kept repeating the word SURRENDER. In his thick Japanese accent he said, SURRENDER, SURRENDER like a mantra several times over. Unbeknownst to me, I was being taught a spiritual principle. Surrender seemed like a great concept, but I hadn't a clue as to its deeper meaning. After Reuho left, taking my migraine with him, I got dressed and headed off to collect Amber and grab a bite at the Café Flore before our show rehearsal.

After a year of his drug experimentation, Reuho, in my opinion, was beginning to lose his purity. He found himself indulging in stronger and darker drugs and one day he took an overdose of Angel Dust and had a psychotic breakdown with violent eruptions. Shirley had to call in the troops for help when Reuho chased her around the apartment with a knife. To avoid hospitalization, we took turns sitting vigil with him as he went in and out of a coma for more than forty-eight hours. When it was my turn to watch over him, I sat on the end of the couch where he lay curled up in the fetal position. Like a baby, he put his head on my lap and took one of my hands in his two strong hands and while in a semi-conscious state began to apply deep Shiatsu pressure into the palm of my hand. I stroked his hair and he nuzzled deeper into my lap. I had never entertained sexual thoughts about Reuho before because I did not want to destroy the purity of our relationship, but suddenly I felt aroused. I tried to slip out from under his head and as I did this; he grabbed my middle finger and started to pull it backward as if he wanted to snap it off my hand. I got very frightened of his strength and was able to slip through his grip and move away from him. And the whole time he appeared to be asleep.

Reuho survived this breakdown, and he and Shirley eventually married. Not long afterwards, his elder brother, who at that time had inherited the role of head priest of his family's temple, died suddenly, and when Reuho went back to Japan to attend the funeral, the temple's board members implored him to come back to Japan and take over the temple. Shirley joined him as his temple wife; he shaved his head, and followed his destiny.

37

Jail Bird

On the same day that Reuho took away my migraine and taught me the principle of surrender, I got dressed and headed off to collect Amber and grab a bite at the Café Flore before our show rehearsal. Feeling hopped up on the healing energy and caffeine, I pulled away from my parking place and made an illegal U-turn in the middle of Market Street to get going in the right direction. In my rear-view mirror I caught a glimpse of a cop as he almost fell off his bike making a quick turnaround to catch up with me, but I kept on going. Amber begged me to stop, but I felt invincible. In the back of my mind, I knew that if he stopped me, he would check my license and find my outstanding traffic warrant.

When the motorcycle cop finally caught up and waved me over, I remembered Reuho's message and surrendered. With my brain firing off excuses, he pulled in front of my VW Bug and made the hand gesture to roll down my window. I played innocent and pretended I hadn't seen him chasing me. He asked me for my license and registration.

"I left my purse at home," I lied. He asked me to get out of my vehicle.

Amber was batting her eyes at the cop trying to distract him.

"Officer, what did my friend do?" she said in her sex-kitten voice.

The cop noticed my gigantic purse on the car floor. "What's in that big purse?" the officer asked. Then he ordered me to get the bag and dump the contents on the hood of my car. I repeated that I didn't have any ID as he picked up my wallet and scrutinized my California driver's license with my smiling photo.

The officer asked, "Who's this in your picture?"

"It's my sister, we're twins and we have identical purses and I grabbed hers by mistake this morning."

"Are you a gypsy?"

"What makes you think that?

"Because all gypsies lie."

Although I knew this was not the surrender Reuho had in mind for me, I had to laugh at the irony. So off I went to the San Francisco City Jail. Luckily it was the first of the month and all my friends on welfare had just gotten their checks. After one phone call, the gossip mill spread the dish that Dolores DeLuxe had been taken to jail as a political prisoner. Before the ink was dry on my fingerprints, a small posse showed up with my bail. I was greeted outside the bars with a Quaalude and was taken directly from the jailhouse to the fabulous Hula Palace where the Grand Princess Lee Lee, a.k.a. Lee Mentley, was hosting one of his fabulous salons. This was the first time Winston Wong performed a piece called *Bound Feet,* for which he later won an Obie Award and before he performed with his punk band, Tuxedo Moon. I felt so privileged to be a part of this community of cutting-edge artists. In the intimate setting of the Hula Palace living room, I sat on the floor spellbound and watched Winston manipulate a handmade puppet to tell the story of oppressed Chinese women. Once again I was reminded of the many ways women have been unjustly imprisoned throughout history and cultures. His artistry breathed life into his magnificent puppet as he spoke volumes without a single word.

A month after this incident, the Boom-Boom Girls were invited to perform at the California Institution for Women, a State Prison in Corona. As our van pulled through the opened gate with the barbed wire all around the facility, I had an eerie feeling in my gut. I was happy to be giving back to this disenfranchised community, but afraid to come so close to real criminals. This was decades before the passing of the three-strikes law, but I felt I was tempting fate after my three brushes with incarceration, once in New Jersey for shoplifting and twice in L.A. for traffic warrants. I got very nervous during the security check. What if they found out I still had some old warrant in the system? Just being in that environment made me guilty.

Once we got past security, I relaxed and we were brought into a recreation room that looked a lot like a school gym with a small stage at one end. The room was set up with round tables and chairs for the inmates to watch the show. While we were preparing back stage, the guards let in our eager audience. From a safe distance, I imagined the worst. What if the inmates were restless and planning a prison break? We would be convenient hostages.

We had prepared one of the early Boom Boom shows in which we played white trash gals at a trailer park looking for love. My favorite song from that show was a clever country western lyric that Janice wrote. As we sang the lyric in four-part harmony, "A beer and a pizza and a man that'll treat ya like the woman he loved as a child," our first and only all-female audience went wild.

When the show ended, the coordinator told us that we would then participate in a meet-and-greet with the inmates. I was reluctant to get down off the stage and as soon as I did, one of my new fans cornered me.

"You were fucking amazing. You gotta come sit at my table, please!" She said.

Reluctantly, I sat down. She was a fast talker with a desperate intensity and within a few sentences I knew her life story.

"I got three young kids on the outside in foster care. When their deadbeat dad left I had to deal weed to make ends meet, "she said.

"How long is your sentence?

"Twenty years."

"For selling dope?" I asked.

"Yeah, that and second-degree murder."

I sat in awe as she went on to defend her crime.

"Because I was inching in on his territory, a rival dope dealer put a hit out on me. It was self defense. I haven't seen my kids in five years, only pictures."

My heart went out to her. At this time the law was cracking down hard on pot dealers, especially poor ones who had no access to deep pockets for their defense. I believed she was telling the truth, and I clearly thought, *There but for the Grace of God, go I.* Her vulnerability touched my heart, and by the end of our time together she asked for my address. She said it would mean a lot to have a friend on the outside.

A month later her letter came. As I read in between the lines it was apparent that she had interpreted my compassion as romantic interest. She signed her letter, "Love and Affection from the Woman's House of Correction." I didn't want to encourage her fantasy, so I never wrote back. I always felt bad about that.

Later that year, Martin Worman wrote a musical about a political prisoner, *The Passion of Barbara Martinez,* and used my prisoner's line, "Love and Affection from the Women's House of Correction," in a song lyric.

38

Free Fall

*B*roken Dishes opened at the Goodman Building in 1976 and over the next year and a half we did short runs at local clubs like The Palms Café on Polk Street where the show continued to evolve with new numbers, characters and back-up boys.

Amber and I played fag hags looking for love at a gay disco with a song added by Patrick Cowley called "Doin' the Discontent." Patrick was the techno musical genius behind all of Sylvester's disco hits. Long before the film *Victor Victoria*, we turned the tables as women playing men, playing women: Amber as a drag version of Cher and me as a drag Bette Midler singing "Beat Around the Bush," a song Martin Worman contributed. Our assaults on female characters raised a few eyebrows among the queens who swung further to the left than we did. I was pretty outraged when I learned that Teddy Mathis, a drag performer I had shared stages with, was drumming up protest against *Broken Dishes*, saying that we were politically incorrect. I dished the queen's criticism with the obvious, "How dare a man, even if he does wear a dress, tell me and Amber—real women and mothers—what the correct political agenda was for our show." Despite the jealous queen's objections, we had a remarkable run.

Along with producing, performing and mothering Viva and the adult children in my household, the years from 1973 through 1977 were a swirl of activities: parties, shows and more parties—along with some Indie-film roles—alternating with hops to Orr Hot Springs and all points north. I made my first silent film appearance in a grainy Super-8 film by Marc Huestis, *Miracle on Sunset Boulevard*. Marc cast me as the Great Goddess bringing peace and enlightenment to the disturbed and aging film diva played by Silvana Nova. Even Viva had a cameo role. Marc later cast both Viva and me in his first serious work, in 1977, *Unity*. This film was a response to the California Briggs Initiative, which would have legislated discrimination against lesbian and gay teachers had it passed. I got to play a gypsy fortune teller with her beggar daughter—played by Viva—in a cabaret scene set in Nazi Germany that told the unknown story of the persecution of gays under Hitler. That same year Marc and Danny Nicoletta founded the Gay Film Festival of Super 8 Films, which eventually became the San Francisco International LGBT Film Festival.

In the Castro, the Café Flore on Market Street was the daily hangout, the place to kick off an average day with the best foamy lattes in town and many friends from the neighborhood. David Baker Jr. lived up the block on Beaver Street, and Beaver Bauer lived around the corner on Noe Street with Rodney, Brain and Sham and other Angels. Everything was in short hops; even the best day spa in the world, the Russian Baths, was located a few doors down from the Café Flore on Market. At the Russian Baths you could get a Finnish Sauna in the public room for two bucks and spend the whole day if you liked. The women's public room was a large space with several levels of wooden benches. It contained a stone sauna that blended the perfect ratio of wet to dry heat. Older European ladies created aroma therapy by placing Eucalyptus branches and grapefruit peels on the sauna, then pouring cold water on the hot rocks to fill the room with herbal citrus steam. Women from all the local communities—gay, straight, young and old, including our children—would hang for hours, alternating hot and cold buckets of water over their naked bodies. The Russian Baths had group and couples rooms as well, so I could share a bath with my male friends in privacy.

Before Lulu moved to the city to be a back-up boy in *Broken Dishes*, he lived at the renowned country spa Orr Hot Springs and was a detox expert. After doing a ten-day Master Cleanse with Lulu, he instructed me to meet him at the Russian Baths to end our fast with a cayenne pepper enema. He thought it was a good idea to do our enemas in the sauna to further help our detoxification process—or as Lulu called it, DE-DISH-I-FI-CATION GIRL! We filled our enema bags to the brim with the spicy warm liquid and as our pores released toxins, we took our enemas simultaneously, forgetting that there was only one toilet available in our private sauna room. Lucky for me, I beat Lulu to the pot. I can still hear his cries, wrenching, yelling and banging from the other side of the bathroom door, GIRL! GIRL! HURRY UP BEFORE I SHIT MYSELF. After his sauna trauma, we moseyed on down the road to the Café Flore for a long-awaited danish and latte.

There was never a dull moment or lack of company to be had in San Francisco. In the mid-'70s, John McGuire and Tim McKenna were more ambitious than any of my other friends, who mostly survived on government subsidies, like SSI and AFDC. As the welfare elite, we believed it was our right and duty to reject the system that waged wars against third world countries and corporations that oppressed poor workers. As artists, we thought it was noble to find ways to make the government pay for our art whether they liked it or not. Many a *scamvestite* loved to quote Miss Holly Woodlawn from an Andy Warhol film, when she fought with her welfare caseworker, "I was born on welfare and I'm going to die on welfare."

John and Tim were the only two gays I knew, except for Harvey Milk, who owned a business on Castro Street. In the summertime, while John and Tim were busy working in the city to afford their new summer house at the Russian River, they would let me stay at the rustic house during the week. They were incredibly generous and didn't even mind if I invited some of my friends to join me.

Once I spent a week there with Viva and David Baker Jr. so that we could do the Master Cleanse in a natural environment without the temptations of the city. It was David's first time fasting but my second go-around with the popular fast. By our sixth day of nothing but water, lemon juice, cayenne pepper and a trace of maple syrup, John and Tim came up on Friday night and decided to throw a party. They had invited a few of my other roommates, too. I went from fast to feast quicker than a New York minute and gorged myself on John's amazing vegetable lasagna and seven-layered chocolate cake. That night David and I took turns clogging up the fragile septic tank plumbing. John never let me forget it.

I also studied Flamenco dance with the renowned Rosa Montoya, a Spanish spitfire no taller than me, but whose stage persona was grand and glorious. She could kill an audience with her speeding-bullet footwork. Although I never aspired to be a serious Flamenco dancer, I got to perform the classic Flamenco dance when my fellow dance student, Walter, a Cuban American who performed with the Angels of Light, invited me to perform with him at a special Angels Cabaret Show. The two of us came up with a killer routine. For the skit preceding our dance number, I created an outrageous character: a Mexican lady who owned a restaurant and hired Walter as her waiter to help stomp out the cockroaches. I dressed in an original Flamenco dress of green and white polka dots that had layers of ruffles trailing behind in traditional style. The dress alone was reason to put on this show, and how I acquired it is a whole other story. Suffice it to say, I took the dress off the back of Grasshopper, one of the most frequently wasted drug users of the Mukluk Manor, another commune of our people. That day, Grasshopper was so out of his mind on PCP that I persuaded him to trade outfits right in front of the Midnight Sun on Castro Street, in broad daylight. I still have the dress to this day, and worked it recently in an Indie movie.

To enhance my character's stature, I secured two pillows under my skirt at the hips so that I appeared almost as wide as I am tall. I did my hair up in a severe Spanish bun, then penciled big wide spit curls to my cheeks. In the skit, I entered the stage with an extra large Black Flag bug-killing aerosol pump spray, and began cursing at Walter in Spanish and English.

"*Pendejo, maricone*, whore, queer, get up off your lazy ass and start killing *las cucarachas*."

Then the music came up and Walter and I broke into a Flamenco dance stomping out the roaches. The hilarious visual of me—four-feet wide by five-feet tall with enormous hips swinging and almost knocking skinny Walter off the stage each time we passed one another—covered up the fact that I was not the best Flamenco Dancer on the stage.

During those years I swung the pendulum from one extreme to the other: Master Cleanse to lasagna; gospel choirs to Devil Slide; double lattes to coffee enemas; disco dancing to yoga—all the while keeping my sights on building my theater career.

Dolores Deluxe and Walter Fitzwater
Mind Kamp Kabaret, August 1976. The Angels of Light Caberet
Photo by Dan Nicoletta

Lulu as Geisha Girl in the Temple of Flowers
Photo by Teena Rosen Albert

Viva as Gypsy beggar with Lulu, still from
Unity, a film by Marc Huestis, 1976

Joe Morocco with Me and Amber as Bette and Cher
Backstage, Mabuhay Gardens, 1977

39

Punk Club

By the spring of 1977 we brought *Broken Dishes* to dinner theatre at the Mabuhay Gardens, a Filipino restaurant on Broadway in North Beach. It was across the street from the much publicized Condor Club, where Carol Doda made waves in the late '60s and early '70s dancing topless and bottomless, and around the corner from *Beach Blanket Babylon,* Steve Silver's drag extravaganza. Showtime was at 8 p.m., and after we took our final bows at 10 p.m., the Filipino restaurant owner turned the stage into the first home for San Francisco's emerging Punk Rock scene. In our shared dressing room, we tripped over punks and undressed in front of head bangers who drew swastikas and rude remarks on the walls and mirrors. The inconvenience was worth it, because the critics were comparing us to the hit show, Beach Blanket Babylon but saying we were by far the better show with original songs and more bite to our satire. Amber and I both earned nominations—along with Debbie Reynolds—that year for best performers in a Musical by the BATCC-Bay

Area Theatre Critics Circle. Debbie Reynolds won, but that was the closest we had ever come to getting mainstream recognition. Riding on this critical acclaim, we decided to spend a month tightening up the show and then reopen in June at the Mabuhay Gardens in time to compete for the tourist dollars that *Beach Blanket Babylon* was raking in.

During the show meeting, our backup boys, Lulu, Tom Waits and AJ Griffin, along with Scrumbly, Marshall and Danny Nicoletta, all gathered to decide collectively on cuts needed to make the show work for a mainstream audience. Amber balked. She refused to cut one precious word from any of her monologues—and then announced that she was quitting the show because it no longer suited her spiritual needs. Everyone was shocked, but no one more than me. We had all worked for free over the past two years, and now that we were finally in a position to make it pay, Amber pulled the rug right out from under us. I wanted to kill her, but instead I went to the beach.

I had sensed a change in the wind before this unhappy ending to *Broken Dishes*. By January of 1977, I moved out of Clayton Street and was living alone with Viva for the first time in a one-bedroom apartment with a spectacular view at the top of Castro and 21st Street. That Easter week, during our dress rehearsals at the Mabuhay Gardens, Viva was almost seven and had come down with the chicken pox. I was full of guilt for having to leave her with a sitter, so I went down to the market on 18th and Castro to pick up a few of her favorite things including eggs to color for her Easter basket. I was rushing to get the shopping done and get home in time to give Viva an oatmeal bath to ease her itching before I had to leave for rehearsals. At the checkout in the market, I remembered Viva's apple sauce, and I rushed back to the aisle to get it. As I lifted the largest bottle off the shelf, it slipped from my hand and crashed to the floor. I turned to look for a clerk to clean up, and, with one step, I slipped and fell. There I lay on the floor impaled by glass and apple sauce. Without making a fuss, I got up and selected another bottle off the shelf and checked out with my groceries.

I carried the groceries a few steps to the corner bus stop and waited for a bus to take me up the three block steep hill to 21st Street. As I sat the heavy bags at my feet, I looked up at the clock on the Bank of America building across Castro and remembered it was Good Friday. It was 3 o'clock sharp; the exact hour according to my early religious teachings, that Christ died on the cross. My thoughts drifted to a scene in *The Greatest Story Ever Told*, a film about the crucifixion: The image of black, ominous clouds rolling over the earth, casting frightening shadows as Magadelene and Mother Mary looked on in anguish as Jesus took his last breath on the cross. At that exact moment, the famous San Francisco fog rolled in over the Castro and ate up the last remaining drops of sunlight that were keeping me warm.

As I waited at the crowded bus stop, all the ghosts of Easters past ran through my mind. I recalled the Easter tweed suit I made on my little Singer sewing machine when I was twelve; then I flashed back to the nuns at St. Anthony's forcing me to my knees to do the Stations of the Cross; then came the memory of that first Easter weekend I spent in Venice with Mark Anthony, the ex-con who stole my mom's Easter gift to me—a gold and diamond chip cross—right off my neck as I slept. This gloomy reverie made me wonder if perhaps the slip and fall accident inside the market was brought on by Catholic guilt—my own personal stigmata—to appease the punishing god of my father.

In the midst of the gay hustle on Castro, I pondered my progressive loss of innocence and all the mini victim dramas I had played out in my less-than-holy life. Just as my pity party was raging in my mind, my ex-roommate, Martin, stumbled out from the Midnight Sun, a popular watering hole at any time of day or night. Martin was sloppy drunk and looked like Judas on a bender. With his long, greasy hair falling in his face, he looked up and noticed me from the distance and started yelling my name.

"Deluxe, girl—Oh girl—GIRL—MISS DELUXE—OH GIRL!"

I thought if I had to hear, "OH GIRL" just one more time I would stab myself. This was just one more nail in my cross to bear. In any other city but San Francisco, a diva of my caliber would not be waiting for a bus in the cold fog to carry her groceries up a steep hill. I was having a very bad Good Friday. The next morning, Holy Saturday, while Christ was hibernating in the tomb, and with the fog still hovering over the City, I awoke from a very strange dream. It was so vivid and so weird that I recorded it in my journal.

A hard driving bass is pumping and Gloria Gaynor is singing "I Will Survive" as I dance on a crowded floor. Gay men all around me pass and snort poppers as the crescendo builds. While spinning, I look up at the disco ball casting sparkles over the gay crowd. The ball spins faster and faster and begins to burrow a hole in the ceiling. As the hole grows larger, I can glimpse into the heavens above. In the sky, a blinding light appears and begins to move rapidly like a meteor picking up speed hurtling toward earth. I'm panicked and try to warn the boys, but no one sees or hears me screaming. The fiery ball keeps coming closer and closer, then crashes down in the middle of the dance floor. Upon landing, the fiery light solidifies into a golden mass shaped like an egg, with light pulsating off of its surface. On shattered glass from the broken skylight, the gay crowd keeps dancing, totally unconscious of the phenomenon in their midst. I grow weary of trying to warn them, so I give up and resume dancing myself. I try to ignore the golden light in the room, too, but it won't let me. The music starts to fade, and the lively action begins to move in slow motion, and then one by one, each man on the dance floor becomes transparent, dissolves and disappears. The music stops and I'm there left standing all alone on the dance floor. Only the golden egg remains, vibrating, and the light begins to fill the entire space. Slowly I approach the egg, the source of this outstanding light. Tentatively, I reach out to it and then gently touch it. As I place my hand on the giant egg surface, it cracks open and hatches a golden Buddha from within.

I woke up from the dream, sobbing.

40

Born Star

After Amber pulled the rug out from under my grand plans, I had it. I did one last show in San Francisco before Viva and I took off for that summer to Venice.

Odd Numbers was a benefit performance at the UC Extension Performance Space at Waller and Laguna. For one night only, we were paying homage to our community's favorite song writing team, Scrumbly Koldewyn and Martin Worman.

At this large space the Angels of Light had run their wonderful *Storybook Extravaganza,* and Janice Sukitis had mounted her hysterical comedy, *Mama,* a play based on her real crazy mother's handling of her dead father's corpse.

This night was a mixed bag of the best of Martin and Scrumbly's favorite tunes from Cockettes days and other shows. Whose idea it was to put Viva in the show, I don't recall, but ever since Viva had first arrived to the City with me at three years old, she had stood patiently in the wings at every performance, like *All About Eve.* She had done her homework, and at seven years old was ready to step into the limelight.

"No Nose Nanook," a sultry blues metaphor for a party gal addicted to "Blow," was a song Mink Stole premiered in *Vice Palace* with Divine. It's the lament of a young Eskimo girl who rubbed her nose off from too much cavorting and too much snorting, and was the song Martin and Scrumbly chose for Viva to reprise for this show. I got busy making Viva the cutest red velour skating circle skirt with a hoodie, and trimmed the whole thing in white faux fur.

I was doing "It's a Scream," a showstopper from *Broken Dishes* that Martin wrote for me. It was the lament of a sacrificial virgin about to be thrown into a volcano to appease the Sun God. But in this number, I was the rebellious virgin trying to escape my fate.

So there I was backstage, putting aside my oversized Sun Headdress to wear the hat of a stage mommy and help Viva get ready for her big debut. I was fretting over Viva's makeup and giving her a pep talk, worried that she'd get stage fright and forget her lyrics. Viva's number was up just before mine.

From the piano, Scrumbly announced the song and Viva stepped out on the big stage to a full house, followed by four backup singers dressed as Eskimos. As she hit her mark under the spotlight, the crowd was already cheering. With all the power and poise of an opera diva, she hit that first note and it was immediately clear that I had a little star on my hands. She belted out those words as if she understood what she was actually singing about. When she reached the bridge, she emphasized the innuendo, singing, *"She rubbed her blubber day and night, and now her nose is out of sight."* The crowd was on its feet cheering and gave the longest and loudest standing ovation as little Viva took her bows. Then I had to follow her. I felt like Mama Rose, taking a back seat to Gypsy Rose Lee. Viva was only seven, but it was obvious to me that my child would no longer live in my shadow.

ACT III

ENDS OF RAVE

41

ROAM Built in a Day

I got an invitation from Bill Franklin to housesit his little beach bungalow in Venice while he went off to Rome for the month of June. The timing could not have been more perfect. I needed the time in the sun and surf to lick my wounds and think about what I would do next after my *Broken Dishes* dreams had been smashed to bits. David Baker Jr. had just returned to San Francisco from his European tour and was happy to take over my apartment in my absence while I skipped down the coast for a spell.

When Bill got back from Rome, I wasn't quite ready to return to the cold foggy summer of San Francisco, so Bill invited me to stay with him until I could find another sublet for July. After his Roman holiday, Bill started going by the name Willy and living part-time as his alter ego, a suave Italian filmmaker. I stepped into the role of his *Juliet of the Spirits*. During that month he was my Fellini, and he taught me Italian while making new recipes he learned in Rome, and he followed me everywhere with his Super 8mm camera. We were both actors in need of representation, so

Willy turned our search for Hollywood agents into a movie titled *Undiscovered*, wherein I played a heroine, finding rejection in Hollywood. Viva, Willy and I were so cozy in his tiny love shack that we could have stayed all summer if it were not for Bill's Latin lover, Lorenzo Bias. Lorenzo felt left out and suspected that I was trying to take his man away from him, especially after Bill took me and Viva home to meet his folks.

I stepped up my search for another sublet and, instead of a temporary place, I found a rental that required me to sign a year lease. It was an ideal house right off the beach on Breeze Ave. David Baker was delighted to take over my lease in the Castro, so I left my furniture, friends and underground celebrity behind. Without blinking an eye I made a permanent move back to my breezy beach life in Venice with my ambition aimed toward Hollywood.

Willy and I both were lucky enough to find jobs in Venice at SPARC, the Social and Public Arts Resource Center. Willy was head of Marketing and I was the event coordinator. SPARC was a newly established nonprofit started by Judy Baca, a popular Los Angeles muralist, and her lover Donna Deitch, my first film director. SPARC was located in the old Venice Jailhouse, an historical landmark of Venice. One night during off hours when Bill and I were working alone he decided he wanted to have sex inside one of the jail cells that had been converted to SPARC's art gallery. When I resisted for fear of getting caught, Bill said, "close your eyes and pretend I'm John Travolta," and then he began to make goofy white-boy Travolta-like disco moves to get me in the mood. He looked more like Dan Aykroyd doing the *Saturday Night Live* sketch of "Two Wild and Crazy Guys."

Once again I had found Saturday night fever in another lover and playmate, and I was happy with my sunny good fortune and a paying job at SPARC. I felt I had made a good choice to move back to L.A. The light that had led me to the City by the Bay had been flickering and I wanted to shine on a larger stage. I was fed up with the non-professionalism that came with the darker side of drugs and sex and the likes of saboteurs like Amber. While some of my peers were slipping deeper into darkness, my growing ambition and parenting responsibilities were increasing, and as Viva got older I moved toward sobriety.

But as I was settling back into Los Angeles, the big fish from the small pond was about to bounce her reality check again.

In Venice I tried to re-create my San Francisco performance experience on the beach while I pursued a legit career in Hollywood. Lulu and other friends would come down to visit, and I met lots of new friends too. I even produced a mini-musical for SPARC, casting Lulu, Willy, his boyfriend, Lorenzo, myself and Debbie, my ex-roommate who had moved right down the block on the beachfront. The SPARC Grand Opening benefit, *Jail House Break* featuring *The New Venice Players* was an instant hit.

Toward the end of the decade, I managed to get a toe in the door of Hollywood. I earned my first Guild card by winning *The $1.98 Beauty Show* hosted by Rip Taylor and produced by Chuck Barris, the infamous creator of *The Gong Show* and *The Dating Game*. I even got to meet the esteemed author Christopher Isherwood and his life partner, Don Bachardy, through Willy.

Willy had become an intimate friend to Bachardy. Chris, a very warm and kind-hearted man, completely embraced Willy as part of their family. Because Willy considered me his family, Don and Chris extended their friendship to me. Don also invited me to sit for him one afternoon at his studio where he created two amazing portraits of me that he added to his body of work.

In those first few years back in Venice, it was impossible to stay away from my beloved community in

San Francisco. I went up for every show opening. Shows like *Strange Fruit,* or performances of *The Four Beauties,* with Tommy, Lulu, Theresa and Tina, and *Crimes Against Nature* by the Gay Men's Theatre Collective kept me going back. I even appeared in a new *White Trash Boom-Boom* skit; a spoof on *Crimes Against Nature,* which we called *Crimes Against Theatre,* a love slap to our gay brothers. Martin Worman and nine other men, including Tommy, David Baker Jr., John Sokoloff and Chuck Solomon, had collectively created this hit about faggots and survival, reminiscent of Brechtian tragicomedy.

It was during the rehearsals for the Boom-Boom girl's parody that I aborted the pregnancy created on my date with John, one of *Crime's* comrades to see *Looking for Mr. Goodbar.* While my comrades in *Crimes* were exorcising their homophobic demons, I used my abortion as inspiration for my bit in the parody, *Crimes Against Theater.* I came up with a piece about a very girly girl who was insecure about her femininity. This was a spin on David Baker's monologue in the original *Crimes,* in which he played out his male insecurities with an obsession for jockstraps. In my piece, I wore a tutu made of sanitary napkins and ended my monologue by giving birth to a pillow with a Happy Face on it. Once the pillow was out of me, I threw it at John, my aborted baby's daddy, sitting in the front row cheering me on. It was my way of telling him he was off the hook.

By the end of the glorious decade of the '70s the party drugs of pot, acid and other psychedelics had escalated to heavier substances. Cocaine was not cheap like pot, and therefore only certain people were invited to share. I hated the attitude that cocaine brought to the party, and I found myself abstaining more and more.

These final years leading up to the '80s were racked with tragedy in San Francisco. On November 18, 1978 the shocking announcement that 408 American citizens had committed suicide at a communal village they had built in the jungle in Northwest Guyana. The community had come to be known as "Jonestown." The dead were all members of a group known as "The People's Temple" of San Francisco which was led by the Reverend Jim Jones. It would soon be learned that 913 of the 1100 people believed to have been at "Jonestown" at the time had died in a mass suicide. Just nine days later on November 27th 1978, San Francisco Supervisor Harvey Milk and Mayor George Moscone were killed by former disgruntled supervisor Dan White.

By May of 1979 Dan White received a slap on the wrist as a result of his famous Twinkie Defense. When the verdict was announced all hell broke loose. Five thousand angry citizens gathered at City hall in an event known as the White Night Riot. I had never been a strong activist like my friend Danny Nicoletta, who worked tirelessly at Harvey's camera store and on his campaigns. Other friends also fought hard against the Briggs Initiative with its agenda to ban gays from teaching in California schools, but for the most part my performance community lived our politics on stages. Drag queens like Lulu and others did camp parodies of Anita Bryant, who supported Briggs, to spread awareness of her hate propaganda. Harvey had loved us and we loved him, and there was never a Castro Street Fair that we did not participate in. With Harvey's murder, and these historic events a dark shadow was cast over our gay City. On that night of the White Night Riot while all my friends hit the streets in outrage, I sat home back in L.A. feeling powerless as I watched the news on my television.

In that dark November, when I was still reeling from all the tragedy, I learned that my friend, Bob Reccio, was found stabbed to death by a trick he picked up in a bar. Bob had built props and costumes for *Broken Dishes* and, as many of my theater friends did, he returned to New York by the end of the decade. I remember how shocked I was when I got the sad news, and yet not surprised. Having lived through my own rape and abuse from strangers in bars, I always worried about my close gay male friends who played dangerously.

Venice World Players 1978, from left to right, Debbie Trent, Me, Lorenzo Baez, Bill Franklin, Lulu

42

More Dick

By the end of the decade, Ronald Reagan was running for president and the screws were tightening on the welfare elite, so I took a waitress job at the Lafayette Café, a Venice landmark on the Boardwalk.

During my morning shift, Richard Lambert skated off the boardwalk into a booth in my section. His smiling green eyes looked up from the menu and as he brushed his sandy hair from his eyes and, with a slight southern accent, he ordered chorizo and eggs. Sitting across from him was Jason, his friend, who I barely noticed once I locked eyes with Richard, who preferred to be called by his nickname, Dick. He was flirty and heaped on the charm each time I went over to fill his cup. He drank more of the Lafayette rotgut and remained way past the morning rush. I wondered why this gorgeous straight guy was being so friendly to me. By the time he paid the check, he asked for my number, left a very generous tip and then he and Jason rolled out of the cafe.

I had by then given up my romantic notion about Willy and thought that this could be the Universe gifting me for making a conscious effort to open up to straight men again. The next day, Dick called.

"Hi, this is Dick, the guy from Lafayette's. You remember me?" he asked.

"Wow, I didn't think you would really call, I said.

"I hope I didn't catch you at a bad time, but I'm home with a cold and thought it'd be nice to get to know you some."

"I'm not busy," I said. With that Dick went on to interview me, asking me my likes and dislikes. At first I thought he was shy and trying to build up courage to ask me out on a date, but over a two-week period and several phone conversations, I learned his history.

"Daddy was a coal miner. I didn't want none of that life. I left West Virginia the day after I graduated from high school."

I didn't see Dick for almost a month, but he just liked to talk a blue streak on the phone. I thought it odd, but by our fifth conversation he confessed he was a recovered heroin addict and was getting over Hepatitis B and that's why we had not gotten together yet.

By the time I finally sat in a booth across from Dick, I had already realized that he was not as straight as I had hoped. During that conversation, he shared details about his bisexual relationships. He had ended a three-year relationship with a woman who had aborted his child, which sent him back to men and to Jason, his current lover. During the next few months, I gave up on the idea of finding a straight man and hung out with Dick almost daily. Jason was rarely included in any of our time together, and before I knew it, Dick ended his relationship with Jason and was moving into a place just two blocks away from me.

Dick was in great physical shape—a runner, cyclist and skater—and he made me want to keep up with him. His smooth, hairless, elongated but not overly big muscles and abs were an inspiration. Besides being my workout buddy, a Gemini true to form, he could be just the opposite, a great enabler of my dysfunction. Whenever I fell off my diet and couldn't get off the couch, he'd bring me cookies and ice cream. I could share every detail of my failed diets and he would listen attentively without judgment. As he sat across the couch over the drone of the TV, I could feel him unconditionally loving me. He was homespun West Virginian good sense mixed with street savvy from his past drug-addicted years, and an expert on our mutual self-destructive natures. The longer I knew him, the more I understood his need to take care of people. As long as there was someone—a bigger mess than himself—he had a purpose. He seemed most alive when coming to my rescue—and when didn't I need rescuing?

Dick, usually shy around my theatrical friends, allowed me to drag him to a comedy improv class one night. He surprised me when he got up to do an improvisation and floored everyone with his zany dark humor.

After being best friends for over a year, Dick invited me to his office Christmas party. He wanted me along because he knew how boring the office geeks at his data-processing job would be, and yet he didn't want to be rude by turning down their invitation. From the minute Dick picked me up, he started treating me like I was a real date. He was an innocent country boy, wearing his best Sunday duds, cowlick slicked down with hair grease, out to impress his girl. When Dick opened the car door for me, I felt like the ingénue Lori in *Oklahoma* when Curly escorted her to the social in the "Surry with the Fringe on the Top." As the evening went on, I could tell he was seeing me in a different light. By the end of the night, the inevitable happened, and it was glorious.

I should have known better because he was a Gemini, and in spite of my extensive knowledge on the subject, I still woke up the next morning swirling in expectations. We were so compatible, and he had told me on more than one occasion that he felt more complete in his relationships with women, plus we were already best buds, and now great sex was added to the stew. What more could a girl ask for? It didn't take long to realize that that's not what Dick had in mind at all.

Over breakfast the next day, Dick said, "You know that cute guy George from your improv class? He gave me his number, but I lost it. Can you get it for me? I think he is super hot."

Once again I was hurled into the depths of hell and found myself in prayer, asking for release from this painful unrequited desire. My prayer was answered and within the next twenty-four hours I fell back into our unconditional true love, free from expectations that remained throughout our friendship.

43

Guru

On New Year's Eve 1980, at the stroke of midnight, I found myself fleeing from a desperate comic who was trying to kiss me. I didn't want to start the decade off with a loser. On the surface I was breaking into films and television, while below the surface a virus was spreading that would explain the mystery of my disco dream I had back in 1977.

"I told Jesus it would be alright if He changed my name" was a lyric Roberta Flack sang that I listened to religiously. According to the Aramaic language, the original language of the Bible, the words name and nature are synonymous. This song is taken from a Bible story about the Samaritan woman who recognizes the Messiah and gives Jesus permission to change her name. In essence she is saying that she is ready for the leap in consciousness that comes with being initiated to Christ's way. As the song goes on, Roberta sings the Biblical quote, "The world won't know you child if I change your name. I told Jesus it would be alright if He changed my name." Dolores DeLuxe was preparing to have another name change.

After doing a small role in the indie cult classic, *Repo Man,* directed by Alex Cox, and winning the title of *The $1.98 Beauty Show,* it was time to join the Screen Actors Guild. I decided to change my name for the sake of the Italian mama roles I hoped to play. With one foot still in the Underground and the other in Hollywood, I thought it important to find a name that could work in both camps. I figured if I dropped the 'x' out of DeLuxe and added a 'c' to become DeLuce, it would do the trick. In Italian my new last name, "De Luce," means "of light." Dolores DeLuce literally translates to "Sorrows of the Light" and with this minor practical name change, unbeknownst to me, I was giving the Universe permission to change my name and nature.

On June 1st, 1980, after three years on Breeze Avenue, I moved a few short blocks further north up the Speedway to Paloma Avenue, the street named for Peace. Paloma Avenue is the most luscious of all the walk streets in Venice. It is lined with Jacaranda trees. In June they were in full bloom with a canopy of lavender blossoms. Bougainvillea spilled over the neighbors' fences and trailed the walkway like a bride's train dripping fuchsia blossoms on the path. My new home was in a spacious, light, two-bedroom apartment on the second floor of a duplex, a stone's throw from the ocean with a magnificent clear view of the Pacific.

Once again I took note of a new pattern of threes showing up. My friend Tommy's last name was Pace (the Italian word for peace), my good friend Eugene's last name was Peace, and there I was living on Paloma (the Spanish word for dove—the symbol of peace).

"Give up acid and learn to meditate." A directive voice gave me specific instructions loud and clear while I soaked in a hot tub, coming down from my very last LSD trip in

1976. I had practiced yoga since 1974 when I met Swami Shiva Lingam, but the act of silence eluded me. I read spiritual books and met the popular gurus of the time. I even tried Chaotic Meditation taught by Bhagwan Shree Rajneesh, and T.M., but never found one that worked. The closest I had ever come to accepting a guru came through a book I read in 1974 by Yogananda, *The Autobiography of a Yogi*. But it wasn't until that first day in June of 1980 that Yogananda's words took hold. On the same day I moved into Paloma Avenue, I rediscovered Yogananda's book in a box while unpacking. As I pulled it out, that old inner voice spoke up again, "Oh good, maybe this can lift me out of this mundane experience," it said. The mundane experience my inner voice was addressing was the worst flu ever, brought on by the stress and exhaustion of moving. In the midst of chaotic unpacked boxes, I propped myself up on pillows with the mattress still on the floor to take a rest and opened the book at random. I came upon a chapter titled "Finding Your Teacher." Yogananda's message to the spiritual seeker in this chapter is that it is not necessary to seek your teacher, but that the right teacher would find his student—but only when that student was ready. I didn't think I was ready, nor was I looking for a teacher, but I read on. At the end of that chapter, I fell asleep and had an interesting dream.

In my feverish dream, *I am in Manhattan, partying with my San Francisco friends from the Ranch who had since moved back to New York. Once the hard-core drugs came out, I decided to leave and take Viva back to the small apartment on Houston Street on the lower Eastside where we were staying.*

After putting Viva to bed I heard a loud knock coming from the outside door a few feet from my room. When I was leaving the party, my old show pal Joe Morocco told me he'd be stopping by. Assuming that the buzzer did not work, I went into the hall to answer the knock. In place of Joe was a wild-looking black man holding a broken bottle in his hand. When our eyes locked, he lunged toward me with the bottle, but I slipped past him and ran out into the street. I did this to avert him from my room where Viva was sleeping. He began to chase me, and as I ran, the street grew darker and more desolate. Just as he was gaining on me, out of nowhere, a fancy Lincoln Continental pulled up to the curb and the man behind the wheel offered me a lift. I was afraid to get into the car with this stranger, a handsome, African American man in an expensive suit and hat. My mind told me that a man looking that fine in a fancy car in that neighborhood could only be a pimp, but I saw no other option, so I leaped into his car. I slammed the door shut just as the shadowy figure chasing me caught up with us and the car pulled off. Once safe inside the car, I sensed a powerful peaceful energy emanating from this stranger. The man drove me back to the apartment without saying a word. He walked me into the room where I had left my daughter unattended. Once inside, I found my friend, Judy Brewer, looking after Viva, who remained sleeping. Judy greeted the stranger by his name, James, and when I asked her how she knew his name she replied, "Because he's a Premie." And then I woke up.

It was Saturday, the day after I had the dream, and Viva's dad came to pick her up for the weekend. I was still feeling sick, but feebly managed to continue my efforts to get settled in to our new home when I heard a knock on my door. I wasn't expecting anyone. When I opened the door, my old friend Jamian from San Francisco was standing in my hallway, accompanied by a 6'2" African American bodybuilder. Both men stood topless, glistening and dripping in oils. I couldn't help notice the contrast between Jamian—a fair, skinny blond with flowing long locks—and his larger-than-life companion, whose biceps, triceps and quadriceps were the size of small mountain ranges. The couple brought to mind Fay Wray and King Kong on the top of the Empire State Building.

Jamian had only recently moved to South Pasadena and his roommate was Judy the woman who had appeared in my dream the day before. Surprised to see him, or to see anyone for that matter since no one knew I had moved, I asked, "How did you find me here on Paloma?" and Jamian replied, "Girl, I have my ways." He just happened to be in Venice with his new boyfriend, the ex-Mr. Universe and they were on a break from judging a body building competition down at Muscle Beach.

Seeing Jamian jogged my memory of the dream since he and his roommate Judy had been followers of the same guru since the late '60s. Neither of them had ever shared much about that part of their lives with me. And even if Jamian had, I don't think I would have taken him seriously. The Jamian I was most familiar with was a pure hedonist, a raging queen with a proclivity for big scary muscle men and fist fucking.

I casually mentioned the dream I had with Judy in it and particularly the part about the stranger James, who Judy called a Premie. Then Jamian explained the meaning of Premie. He said it was a Hindi word that meant *lover of the Lord* and that it was what the followers of his guru called themselves. He sat across from me, and looked me dead in the eye, and in his queenly affected manner said, "Girl, that was Guru Maharaji and he came to save you!"

The cynical Dolores DeLuxe, thought, "yeah right," but the new emerging Dolores of Light took note. In less than twenty-four hours, two representatives of some guru I never heard of, one on the dream plane, the other in the flesh, had shown up at my new home on the street named for Peace, and I hadn't even sent out a change-of-address notice.

The next day, with Viva still at her dad's, I decided to rid myself of the clutter with a yard sale just outside my

door. I was still sick with very low energy and my friend
Grace from down the block offered to help. By the end of
the day, I was feeling better and, while packing up, Grace
and I made plans to see a movie at eight.

As I was changing for the movie, I got a call from
Cindy, my friend who had introduced me to Jane Fonda in
1972. I had not seen her in over five years. She asked if she
could stop by for a quick visit. I told her I didn't have much
time, but she insisted since she was right down the street at
the Rose Café and would only pop in for a few minutes.

When she showed up I barely recognized her. The last
time I had seen Cindy was in Berkeley and she had shaved
her head and was spouting her most radical separatist ideas.
But when she appeared in my doorway that second day of
June 1980 she looked younger and more beautiful than she
was back in 1971. Her medium-length light brown hair
framed her soft angelic features and I saw the Cindy I first
fell for when I heard her blow a mean jazz saxophone with
an all girl band in Venice.

"You must have a new lover, you look radiant." I said.

"No, not really. I haven't been with anyone since I left
Berkeley," she said.

"I didn't think you would ever leave Berkeley. Where
are you now?" I asked.

"I live in Miami now."

Miami sent up a red flag. I could not picture feisty
radical Cindy living in laidback Miami, home of half the
countries retirees. This was still a time before Miami had
become the cool, hip South Beach we know today.

"Are you playing with a new band there?" I asked.

"No, I work in a health food store," she answered. The
twenty questions could have gone on before I got any
pertinent details about her current situation, but I didn't
have the time. She then reluctantly said, "My guru lives
there. I practice meditation now."

I knew this had to be one powerful guru to convert this lesbian separatist. Five years earlier, she wouldn't even talk to a man, and now she followed one to Miami. She didn't want to talk about it, but I kept prodding her for details. She finally told me the guru's name. It was the same guru that Judy and Jamian shared. Then I told her about my dream, and she offered to take me to a video presentation that evening to learn more about her guru.

The reluctant seeker in me was just open enough to know this was no coincidence, considering the message I read in Yogananda's book, followed by the mystical trinity of appearances by this guru's followers, first in the dream, and twice on my doorstep. Again, the mystery of the threes; it must have been happening for a reason. I told Cindy I would like to go at a later date since I had previous plans with my friend Grace. Just then, Grace called and said, "Do you mind if I cancel? Larry just got home a day early from his business trip."

That night, Cindy brought me to meet my perfect master. The minute I walked into the hall, the first person I bumped into was Judy. She was so surprised to see me there! As Cindy and I took our seats, I recognized the very man in my dream that had saved me from my dark pursuer. He was sitting at few seats away from us. Later, I learned his name was in fact James, and he too was a follower of the guru.

When I saw their guru talking on a large video screen, I instantly recognized him. He was a radiant, Buddha-like being who resembled the golden statue I had first seen inside the illumined egg that fell from the sky in my disco dream. Except this golden Buddha was not a statue. He was a living, breathing, chubby jester who had me laughing and then crying tears of joy before the night was over. Throughout the evening's presentation, I felt the same protective energy that I had glimpsed throughout my life, both in dreams and in my more spiritually awakened moments like after giving birth to Viva. It was the same presence I felt days after I survived my violent rapist and at the other critical turning points in my life. Just a few weeks after that night, I received the Knowledge techniques from my Golden Guru. It wasn't Jesus, but a change of name and nature had occurred and I began to understand the truth in the gospel as sung by Roberta Flack: *"And Jesus said, the world won't know you child if you change your name."*

From that moment of initiation, without intention, I was struck celibate. My need for love on the outside was replaced by a deeper source of pure unconditional love. Many of my friends thought I was lost in spiritual madness. I tried to describe the feeling: "It's like getting a thousand standing ovations from the Universe," I said as I watched them roll their eyes. While some of my friends dished me, I walked around in a constant state of bliss, but as I went deeper within this protective bubble of peace and love, my playmates were still outside, looking for love in the bars, the bushes and the bathhouses. The very men who had been sleeping with me kept sleeping around with other men, and a dark demon—first identified as the gay cancer—was spreading among them.

44

Last Acts

I met Jane Fonda for the second time while directing a school production of *You Can't Take It with You*. Both Viva and Jane's daughter, Vanessa, had significant roles in the production, and Jane came to the theater every night of dress rehearsals and performances to help Vanessa get ready to play the Russian count. In this middle-school production at SMASH, The Santa Monica Alternative School House, we had few boys to fill the male roles, so I got the girls into drag. Jane patiently helped Vanessa glue hair on her chest to complete her male character. I reminded Jane of our original meeting back in 1972 and told her how she had inspired me to make changes in my life.

In the early '80s I started Tell Mama, a personal-service business for every odd job I could do for cash, offering services from A to Z. While passing out my flyers at the Rose Café to advertise my new business, a successful writer friend took one look at my concept and the caricature of me on the flyer with the list of odd jobs I performed, from ADVICE to ZIPPER REPAIR, and commented, "It would be easier to write the sitcom." To which I replied, "Don't you dare!"

I ran home and wrote the pilot and registered it with the Writer's Guild.

During the eighties, I earned the title of Miss Alternative L.A. as well as The Knitter to the Stars by creating hand-knit, fashions for the actresses and models in my acting class that were booking big commercial jobs. I became a part-time housekeeper and cook for Dean Martin, and juggled commercial auditions and fittings for celebrities like Rose Anne, Fran Dresher, Julia Roberts, Ellen Burstyn and Lily Tomlin.

In 1986 Viva turned sweet sixteen and everyone from her school friends to her gay aunts and uncles—including her only straight uncle, my younger brother, Richie, who had since moved to Hollywood to pursue acting—were at her party. More than fifty guests squeezed into my two-bedroom apartment on Paloma Avenue. Teenagers were breakdancing on the hardwood floors in the dining room as I ran around hosting and making homemade pizza for all.

John Stagliano, aka Butt Man in the XXX world was one of my clients who I had invited. I met John in a dance class and he hired me as his personal assistant/costume designer/set decorator for his X-rated films. John was also a Chippendales dancer and he showed up dressed as Dracula and decided to surprise the birthday gal with a striptease number. Since he was one of my best-paying clients, I couldn't refuse his gift. Viva and her girlfriends sat in a corner laughing at the old straight guy trying to perform his tired sexy moves on them. After her party, Viva threatened me, "Mom, one of these days I'm going to write a book about you and call it *Mommy Queerest.*"

In the midst of life's peaks and valleys, I started to lose the first of my closest friends to AIDS. One by one, my gay boys began to disappear, just as my disco dream prophesized.

"Have I Stayed Too Long at the Fair?" was one of my favorite Streisand songs since I heard it in the '60s. But as often as I played that record, I never heeded its warning. I lived for the fair. Like a hot air balloon, I floated way above the humdrum world, convinced that I'd never come down. But that day had come. One by one, all the jesters were disappearing. The merrymakers were busy going back and forth to hospitals for radiation and blood transfusions. The brakes locked on the merry-go-round and the showgirls were flung onto respirators. No longer safe, I found myself alone at the fair.

In 1988 I unintentionally put my stage career to rest with a new show, *The Last Dance of the Couch Potatoes*. At that time, the irony in the show's title escaped me. I wrote a more-than-ambitious three-character multimedia musical comedy about an agoraphobic shut-in addicted to television and junk food, and then played the lead role and more than a half-dozen fantasy characters that were figments of my character's imaginings induced by overindulgence in caffeine, nicotine, sugar and media. Because I got dizzy from smoking on stage during rehearsals, I started smoking again for the sake of my character. I'd been nicotine-free for twenty years. The cigarette smoke and the one-minute costume changes in between scenes and musical numbers didn't kill me—but the critics did.

Miss Alternative LA with the judges,
Edie Massey and Weird Al Yakovitch to my right, circa 1980

45

Time Less

With hindsight, I can clearly see that many of my performances and dreams predicted future events. In 1974, during the Gay Pride Parade, glitter rained on the floats of San Francisco's finest, balloon-titted queens while a dark dirge of campy widows dressed in black, '40s-style dresses, seated on the back of a flatbed truck, moved in slow motion through the gay streets. Our theatre troupe, Warped Floors, had earned its reputation for countering the counterculture, and that year we outdid ourselves. I even dressed Viva in black rags to play the part of the poor, orphaned child of the Gay Widows. I don't recall who gets credit for the theme of that parade float, but on the morning of Gay Pride day, either Jorge or Joe Morocco watched one of their roommates waving good-bye to a trick. He made the comment, "Girl, don't you feel like a Gay Widow after a meaningless one-night stand?" That was all it took for us to don ourselves in our best black and put on our tragedy masks. Against the Technicolor backdrop of the parade that year, as we moved through the crowd, waving our hankies and weeping crocodile tears, our little theatre troupe stood out like an ugly blemish on prom night. From under our veils, we spoke out loud, staged whispers: "Thank you for coming, it would have made him so happy."

If we had known we were prophesying our own futures, would we have chosen more wisely or dreamed a different dream?

In the spring of 1988 I was in the middle of previews for *The Last Dance of the Couch Potatoes* at the Powerhouse Theater in Venice when I got a call from Tommy's caretakers. They warned me that it might be too late, but if I hurried there was a chance I'd get to see him one last time to say goodbye. It had been six months since we'd been together, but I talked to him almost daily as he began his intense decline. After a dramatic flight, not unlike the one Bette Midler took in the movie *Beaches,* I rang the bell at his little home on Wilmot Street. After the frightening thoughts on that flight, the last thing I ever expected to see was Tommy rising up from his deathbed to answer the door while his caretakers lapped up some rare San Francisco sunshine in the backyard—but that's exactly what happened.

Tommy came out of his coma just in time for my visit. There he stood in the doorway, no longer the handsome gent pursing his lips and flipping his hair like a girl. My friend was covered in the armor of AIDS-related infections. Tommy resembled a beast I saw in a dream about him ten years before. The only areas of his flesh left unravaged were his beautiful fine hands and feet. I sat at his feet and held them as he tried to get comfortable on the couch. He refused his morphine drip so that he could fully take in these last moments. We both knew this was the end for him, but we never spoke of it. Instead we talked about the wonderful drag shows and juicy dish.

With a raspy voice he said, "Girl, remember that night in the pouring rain when you forced me to climb into a dumpster to find your frigging castanets?"

"Well, who told you to throw them out?" I said.

"If I didn't clean out your funky-ass car, who would?

I wanted to cry, but he could still make me laugh.

During our pasta binges Tommy used to say, "Girl, we have enough pasta in our systems now that when we die, we can donate our bodies to the Golden Grain Company for recycling."

Despite the fact that Tommy had the worst case of K.S. lesions I ever saw, covering what was once his gorgeous face and body, he was the only AIDS victim I ever knew who never lost an ounce of weight. From his deathbed, when he could no longer eat a bite, he planned menus and I ate enough for the two of us. And when it was finally time for him to let go of his body, all that pasta in his system could not glue him to this planet or to me. On every birthday or holiday, Tommy would send me the biggest, tackiest Hallmark card that read, "To My Loving Wife," and those cards came right up until he left me in August 1988.

Me and Tommy S.F.Pride Day, 1979
Photo Dan Nicoletta

46

Tied Ends

During the two months before Tommy died, I had to dress up and show up for my run at the Powerhouse, and then the extension at the Odyssey Theater in West L.A., and through it all I could feel Tommy dying. When I wasn't on stage, I walked through my days as if my feet were set in cement blocks and I was moving through mud. That same year, I turned myself in to Overeaters Anonymous because I could not stop eating pasta.

With the counterculture casualties mounting, the party became the Memorial. I wrote a performance piece titled "Gay Widow" in which I spoofed a well-known scene from *Chinatown*. In the film, Jack Nicholson, as a tough private eye, interrogates Faye Dunaway while slapping her repeatedly. With each slap, Faye changes her response— "She's my sister, my daughter, my sister, my daughter, my sister, my daughter..."—revealing that the woman in question was a result of incest Faye's character suffered at the hands of her powerful, corrupt father.

In my camp rendition, I slapped my own face, chanting, "He's my sister, my mother, my brother, my sister, my child, my husband, my lover." The lost boys were the stars in my show. They had helped to form the woman I had become. At the end of my piece, I raised my glass: "To fags, hags, drags and performance junkies, art, love and drug addicts alike. Children lost in a diseased society who found one another, like ugly ducklings they glided on swan territory and for a brief moment got to shine. Here's to the misfits, the queers, the outcasts, the freaks, my friends."

The same year we lost Tommy, only two weeks later, Rodney Price from the Angels of Light passed. Then Divine and Sylvester died a month apart.

Divine was the fairy godmother that turned me into the Pumpkin that led to my rebirth on stage in 1973. In my last phone conversation with Divine, a few months prior to his unexpected death, we discussed our concerns for mutual friends who were infected with the virus. I never imagined I had to worry about Divine, my larger-than-life mother/mentor/friend. His love and humor were my greatest teachers, and when he made a sudden departure from this world, it was a real shock. I think his heart was way bigger than those fake tits he flaunted, and just too big not to break; when it did, he followed after the lost boys into Never-Never Land.

Next to being a movie star, Divine always wanted to be a mother. And to me, she was. In the John Waters film *Pink Flamingos*, the Egg Lady, Edie Massey, was Divine's mother. By the '80s, Edie had moved to Venice and ran a small antique shop on Abbott Kinney Blvd. When I entered the Miss Alternative L.A. Contest hosted by the Landmark Theatres, Edie was one of the judges. When Edie cast her vote for me, she proclaimed in her squeaky little girl voice, "I like her the best because she looks just like a baby Divine." When I beat out a dozen real drag queens for the title, Edie gave me my crown. Edie's public recognition of my true lineage to Divine was the best part of winning the contest.

By the mid '80s, my sweet friend John McGuire had become a successful L.A. interior designer and lived with his partner, Winston Wilde, on his ranch in Malibu. He was closer than a brother to me, and Viva and I were always included in every one of his large family gatherings. When Sylvester died, John offered to fly me to Oakland with him to pay homage to our mutual friend at his memorial at the Oakland Love Center.

John and I held hands as we joined the procession of Sylvester's family, friends and hundreds of fans. The event was reminiscent of our days at the Black Gospel Churches as hats, furs and fans were flying and many were testifying—but no one louder than the deceased himself. Sylvester's falsetto tones rang out, loud and clear, over the cries and shouts of the congregation as we stomped and shouted to his biggest hit, "You Make Me Feel (Mighty Real)". As we approached the church altar with the open casket on display, John gripped my hand. There Sylvester lay in all his glory, every last detail selected by his own hand: Red lips to match the red oriental silk kimono, gold eye shadow to highlight the brocade stitching. It couldn't get any realer than that.

A few short years later, when John had his first major AIDS related setback, I got to rescue him. I climbed in his hospital bed and held him as he lay shivering after an invasive medical procedure. At the end of his days, John went back to Seattle to be in the nurturing arms of his big loving family. A week before he passed, I got to have a long phone conversation with him. I remained close to John's mom, his sister Mary, and his two gay brothers, Pat and Jim. Every time I hear a gospel choir, I feel it's John visiting me from beyond the grave.

As I buried several of my gay husbands, my dad prepared for his exit, too. The year before he took ill, on a trip back East, I took my dad and brother to see my guru speak at Radio City Music Hall. Dad had forgotten his hearing aid and was struggling to hear the message, but afterwards he expressed his amazement at seeing so many people with the gift of faith. As we rode the elevator down to the parking level, Dad confided in me that he did not believe in God, and that he feared his death. In that crowded elevator, Dad put his arms around me and said, "You know, I always admired your courage. I wish when I was young I could have been more like you. In those days it was different. I'm sorry I didn't do right by you."

"Dad, we both hurt each other. I know we didn't mean to. Those years led me to have faith. I forgive you Daddy, and I hope you can forgive me and yourself too."

I told him I'd pray he'd find faith.

A week before my father passed, I flew home just in the nick of time to rescue Dad from the cancer ward where I found him tied down in a straight jacket. The nurse said it was the only way to prevent him from pulling out his IV drip of chemo. I insisted that they let him loose and I spent that night in the ward with him until I could arrange to have him released to home hospice.

With the odor of antiseptics and retching sounds of pain, I dozed off sitting bedside through the night. In a fitful sleep, I had a dream in which Bill Franklin appeared and asked me to come home to Venice because he was dying, too. In the dream, I told Willy he would have to wait his turn; I had to help my father die first.

Dad woke me from my nightmare. He was ranting and it took me awhile to calm him. He wanted to get up out of his bed, but he was so weak he could not walk or stand on his own, but he kept insisting. I did my best to lift him up out of bed, and then propped him up against the side of the bed and I held him in my arms so he would not fall. We just stood there swaying back and forth. I said, "Look, Daddy, you always wanted to dance at my wedding, and now we're dancing." He laughed. I gently eased him back into his bed. He lifted his trembling hand and stroked my cheek and told me I was his angel. With the help of my brother we arranged for Dad to come home and a few days later, Daddy passed. I held it together until after his funeral, and then came home to Venice.

I managed to have a month more with my loving Willy. In his final days, he kept asking me what items I wanted after he was gone, and I just couldn't say. It felt too final, but in the end, I asked for his television. Bill put it in his will and allowed me to stay close to him right up until his final curtain.

Dick Lambert, my great enabler and workout buddy, used to shake his head and laugh when I tried to argue my meaning of the Truth. He associated spirituality with his early religion and wanted no part of it. When Dick and I first became friends, I was consumed by my new-found bliss and a bit self-righteous.

"Honey, you took way too much acid in the '70s," he said.

I just never understood how someone with so much Light was so resistant to a Higher Power. His heart was always open and he was a consummate caretaker, but when he needed care in the end, it was difficult for him to accept it, even from me. I believed he could have lasted longer, but he let the hospital kill him quick one night. It was just unbearable for him to need help. He was far more comfortable giving than taking.

Viva and I were together when I got the news about Dick's death. I barely cried, and said to Viva, "If only he'd believed, maybe he'd still be alive." Viva sobbed uncontrollably. She was twenty and had loved him since she was nine years old.

That afternoon, Viva had an audition in the valley for a TV pilot. She was so shaken over Dick's passing that I didn't want her driving, and I didn't want her to miss her audition either, so I played Mommy Strongest and volunteered to drive her. It was a particularly beautiful day for L.A., and as I drove over the Sepulveda Pass with Viva still crying, it dawned on me that I'd never see my friend's youthful firm body or shining face again. I had nothing tangible to hold on to. I never met his family, and I didn't like his other friends. All I had left was one snapshot of Dick standing in his kitchen while cooking my breakfast, wearing white shorts and a green T-shirt—that great shade that brought out the color of his eyes— holding a frying pan as he smiled at the camera.

Yet life for me went on, and the panoramic view of the San Fernando Valley came into sharp focus when I reached the peak of the hill and saw the sky was blue with white fluffy clouds and I inhaled the beauty of life and the earth and hills around us.

Richard Lambert visits me in my dreams and I still see his face as I walk along the beachfront. To this day, I make a point to look up at the window every single time I pass the last apartment where he lived on the Speedway, as if I expect him still to be at home.

Dick Lambert , Venice, 1981

47

More Loss

As a woman living on the edge at the end of time, I
felt more familiar with death than life as I buried
the dead from the mid '80s into the mid '90s.
Coming from a long line of Italian drama queens, I had to
fiercely fight the impulse to throw myself onto the coffins.
I knew better than to expect sympathy for being a middle-
aged fag hag who was losing my lifelong companions and
the people in the straight world I now inhabited just could
never know the depth of my loss.

I wrote this entry in my journal after Bill Franklin died:

I feel like the heroine in the film Poltergeist, *clawing my
way out from a pool of muddy demons. These ghosts
beneath my pool keep dragging me back, pulling me under
the mud. They wish to keep me there as their eternal
companion and I scream for help, for I must live, but I'm so
weary. Why won't they release me? What do they want
from me? Maybe I was not all I could have been for them
when they were still here, and this punishment is the*

promise of the vengeful Father-God of my youth. Should I just surrender and allow them to pull me beneath? Just let go and surrender to what feels like death, or do I hold on to the edge trying for one more breath to sustain me? Nothing comes to mind now. I am blanker than a Barbie on vacation. My breath is looking for a place to release and I am holding. Numb, I pray for a safe place to exhale, but I cannot even sense the surface. I am drowning. Horror of quicksand, darkest slime, so dank, pulls me deeper into the earth. Where's the Mother promised in this dirt? Where's the Father promised in the heaven I hope I am going to?

Janice wrote me a letter after we lost our good friend Joe Morocco:

When Tommy Pace and Rodney Price died two weeks apart, I thought there was something seriously wrong with my choices in life. Tommy died like a devil, angry and alienated, and Rodney died like an angel of light. Rodney and Tommy died so close together and were such good friends that I think of them now as a black and white ice cream sundae. Now Joe has died and I have the feeling that I will be left in this strange Greek Tragedy with the burden to keep them all alive in memory. All my favorites, going, going, gone...until only my enemies remain and I must fall in love with them out of loneliness, telling them about people I remember, some very well, some not so very well at all.

The night after Tommy's memorial, Janice played me the tape of the benefit the community had organized for Tommy, called, *Give Me the Damn Money*. This was a combination fundraiser and a chance for Tommy to attend his own funeral. I had not attended because I was still performing *The Last Dance of the Couch Potatoes*.

During the benefit, Tommy, hideously deformed by KS lesions, had hid himself up in the balcony to watch the show. Rodney Price, frail and close to death himself from his AIDS complications, was the highlight of the show. In a skit that took place in a clinic waiting room, Rodney, in a wheel chair, dressed in a hospital gown, bantered with another AIDS patient, played by Ann Block. The humor built as they began to top each other with a long list of their complicated symptoms. At the end of the funny dialogue, Rodney performed a song, written by Janice and Scrumbly, called "I Have Less Time Than You," and then broke into a magnificent tap dance while still seated in his wheel chair.

The irony was that, in actuality, Rodney had more time than Tommy—but only two weeks. From the audience, you could hear the sobs of Antonia, Tommy's roommate's daughter, a young child, who knew her uncle Tommy was dying. It was by far the most profound evening of entertainment and a send-up to the spirit of this wild community that was losing its best and brightest. That night, Janice and I watched the tape after Tommy's memorial and held each other while taking turns sobbing in a twelve-hour marathon cry. It was the most intimate time I had ever spent with a sister.

Photo booth shots of me and Jan Sukaitis

Gay Widow Dolores and Janice with Viva the Gay Orphan

Gay Widows
Left to right top: Jan Sukaitis, Pristine Condition, Joe Morroco, Archie Connolly. Bottom row: Janet Planet, me, Doug, and Bobby Star

Jimmy Drinkovitch, Venice neighbor and sweetheart

Martin Worman, Cockette/lyricist

Viva & Pristine Condition at the 20 year reunion of the Hulah Palace and the Cockettes. April 3, 1994. *Photo by Dan Nicoletta*

Lelani, circa 1980's pin up days

48

Epilogue

SLAP HAPPY

Last year I spent a day in San Francisco with my friend Phillip, who I have known since 1972. I am always happy to be with my fellow survivors here in this brave new world. Phillip, still a gorgeous, glorious queen in his '50s, has never lost his hair, his looks, his edge or his outrageous style. As we strolled through Golden Gate Park on a Sunday afternoon, past the very spot by the bandshell where I made headlines riding my makeshift dildo chariot, we chatted about days gone, and then caught up on the present.

I told him all about Viva's incredible talent that has led me to take many a fifteen-hour flight for the past decade to exotic locales like Hong Kong, Singapore, Thailand, China and Vietnam—destinations I never imagined I would see at this juncture of my life.

Phillip could take almost as much pride in my daughter's success as I could, since he was one of the creative influences Viva got from our shared journey that led her into dance and acting, and eventually to becoming the gifted jazz and blues singer she is today. I told Phillip all about the first time I arrived in Hong Kong during Viva's hectic life as she was rehearsing with her new band, preparing to travel to Shanghai, and singing six nights a week at various venues throughout Hong Kong. It was the most inopportune time for a visit from Mama, but there I was because it had been almost a full year since I'd seen her, the longest time we had ever been apart, and I missed her.

Her employer, Jamie, a British expat, took an instant liking to me and on my first night there I got to see my daughter perform at the popular 1996 Bar in Lang Qui Fong, the nightclub district of Central Hong Kong, for Gay Disco Night. Although this was a small bar that normally had no entertainment, on Friday's Happy Hour, Jamie would put a platform on top of the bar and Viva would step up on the makeshift stage and sing disco hits by Donna Summer, Ellen Champagne King and Diana Ross while the boys ate her up.

That night, Jamie got up to make his introduction and mentioned my presence in the club. Over the microphone he announced in his thick British accent, "We have a mum in the club tonight; its Viva's mum. We've never had a mum in this club before; let's bring her up to say a few words; let's welcome Viva's mum." Well, it was the first time I was being brought to the stage as the mother of the performer, and little did Jamie or the boys in the house know that this mum was no stranger to performing on bar tops. When I hit the stage, I immediately had a story to brag about my daughter and win the hearts of the audience. I opened with, "I bet you didn't know that Viva is a second generation fag hag." I told them all about Viva as a little girl of seven bringing the house down during her singing début with the infamous Cockettes. The Cockettes were gay legend, and many of the gays in the bar were American expats and knew the history. That night, after Viva's show ended, the boys lined up to meet and greet both mother and daughter. I felt like Judy with Liza as we held court, graciously greeting our fans.

If it weren't for the miracle of the one great choice I made in my life—the decision to bring Viva into this world—I shudder to think what my fate would have been.

After filling Phillip in on all of Viva's adventures and mine, I casually mentioned, "You know, Viva just had her fortieth birthday."

Phillip stopped dead in his tracks and threw his hands on his hips and screamed, "Girl, how dare you bitch slap me into the future."

I took note that it was time to start lying about my daughter's age. Our kind did not think we'd ever see the future. In my heyday, I never imagined life beyond forty, let alone reaching the age of a Medicare recipient with a daughter that old.

In this future of my own creation, I sometimes weep for those glorious days of the seventies. I recently found my old datebooks in the back of a file drawer while doing my 2012 spring de-cluttering. There's the evidence, with every page so full: Show rehearsals, tap, flamenco, yoga classes, parties, parties and more parties. Just going to breakfast with my seven roommates was an occasion to dress to the nines. My cloudy memory tells me that when my life was that full, I didn't take the time to appreciate it. But that's not the truth. I discover from the little notes I left in the margins of those books—notes of gratitude for the joy I felt in the special moments of love and fun. Why did I even save these datebooks? Did I know then that I would need a reminder? Tears make the keyboard slippery as I try to keep my fingers busy so that I can leave a new note of what it's like today, way past the end of an era. Every page contains a name of a friend, now dead, some of whom I had forgotten were gone.

Then I remember to bitch slap myself to this present moment and awaken to everything I am grateful for in this big little life of mine:

With the rhythm of my every breath and the beating of my heart, I hear a Diana Ross disco lyric that keeps repeating in my brain: "I have the sweetest hangover; I don't want to get over."

Virgin Sacrificial Goddess to the Sun
Photo © 1978 dannynicoletta.com

In Memoriam

1978-87

Harvey Milk; Bob Reccio; Don Logan; Michael Harriman; Mark Bliefeld; Patrick Cowley; Jackson Allen; Chuck Solomon; Hibiscus; Timo; Peach; Coco Vega; Jack; Boyd; Jerry Francle; Frank; Lelani; Edie Massey.

1988:

Peter Hartman; Tommy Pace; Rodney Price; Divine; Sylvester.

1989:

Jamian Merlin; Bobby Star-Steele; Joe Morocco; Brent Jensen; Merritt Buttrick; Dov; Tim McKenna; Clyde Ventura.

1990:

Dick Lambert; Lorenzo Baez; James Sonoma; Dan Albert; Victor Noel; Ernie Banalis; Michael McCarthy; Rodney White; Pat Daly.

1991:

Dorsey; Jerry Masoni; David Venice-Pitch; Jimmy Evans; John McGuire; Jada; Bodi Wind; Paul Michael Lombardi and Dana Garrett.

1992:

Robert Leal; Sam Hale; Erick Ruttucard; Jimmy Drinkovitch; David Oliver; Doris Fish; Tippy; Bill Hudnut.

1993:

Martin Worman; Archie Connelly; Ken Wilkinson; Tom Fleming; Sando Counts; William Passerelli; Arnie Arnubal; Bobby; Baba Scotland.

1994:

Clifford Olsen; Pristine Condition; John Rothermil; Chuck Smith; Charles Isis.

1995 on:
My Dad; Bill Franklin; Marshall Reiner; David Loud;
David Baker Jr., Fred Pierce, Goldie Glitters; Cockette
Reggie; Russell Clark; Dusty Dawn; Greg Poe.

The Credits

They say it takes a village to raise a child. In the case of this book, it took several villages.

If this were my Academy Awards acceptance speech, I'd be played off the stage before I could name all the names of those who brought me to this moment and this book.

"To fags, hags, drags, performance junkies, art, love and drug addicts alike. Children lost in a diseased society who found one another. Here's to the misfits, the queers, the outcasts, the freaks, my family and friends." I am eternally grateful to each and every one of you.

The Cast
My daughter Viva Vinson; the Grosso Family: Mom, Gloria, Dad, John, sister Ginny, and brother Richie; my nieces and nephew, Danielle, Marco, Sophia; and all of my 50 first cousins; boyfriends and husbands; plus my extended family from Los Angeles to San Francisco, Chicago, New York, Hong Kong and beyond.

Editors

It took a lot to get the girl out of Jersey and the errors out of my manuscript. Fixing the typos and bad grammar of someone who tested at a third-grade reading level in college—due to untreated dyslexia—aint easy.
And the honors go to:
Bo Young, first draft
Amy Friedman, draft two;
Mark Thompson, draft three;
Michael Kearns, drafts four;
Laurie E. Horowitz, final draft;
Mark Mardon for flawless copyediting.

Photography

My two favorite gay husbands, responsible for creating the Diva as you see her throughout the pages of My Life. These men gave till it hurt (in a good way) and contributed generously to our community at large with their brilliant works through the decades.

David Greene for the cover photo and more images throughout the book. DavidJGreene.com

Dan Nicoletta, for his generous photos and constant service and activism and PR wisdom. dannynicoletta.com.

Additional photos by Michael Zagaris, Christina Schlesinger, Judy Baca, Donna Deitch, Janice Sukaitis

Art Director

To Jennifer Lim of "in my house art department," who really got my vision and designed the cover to my delight and the photo layouts within.

Audio Visual

Jean Franzblau for directing and editing the Indiegogo promo video that gave me a financial kickstart; and Betsy Zajko for her final-cut suggestions.

Teachers

To my daughter, Viva, the greatest joy of 'My Life'. Rev. Dr. Michael Beckwith and Rickie Byars Beckwith of The Agape Church. And a very special thanks to my meditation master, Prem Rawat, from whom I learned a way to be in the world but not of the world.

Readers

To my friends with benefits who read early drafts and gave helpful notes along the way and more encouragement than a girl could ask for:
Carol Schlanger, Robert Croonquist, David Greene, Arni Chanin, Laurie Grosso, Edward Vilga, Doris Koenig, Lenore Marquez, Danny Nicoletta, Phil Pollizatto, Jonathan Cainer, Angela Rapkin, Dale Neili, Maxine Nunes, Honey Goldberg, Rob Saduski, John Fleck, Francesca Rosa, and Paula Verbit.

Coaches

Michael Kearns and my "Queer Wise" follow writers; Jenny Laper's Venice writers' Diana, Linda, Grace, Felice; From Amy Friedman's memoir class, Linda Lichtman and Annette Pasternak; Hillary Carlip for encouraging my Gay Widows stories; Wendy Hammers for "Tasty Words"; and Lauri Fraser for "Everybody Loves a Good Story."

Caterers and Craft Service

For all the pasta I could ever eat, my baby bro, Richie Grosso of Giovannie's Ristorante, in Woodland Hills.

Kindness of Strangers
The angels who generously contributed to support the publication of My Life
In Order of Appearance:

LEE MENTLEY
XANDRA COE
MARINA DAY
MIRA CRISP
ED RAK
ROBERT CROONQUIST
RICKIE BYARS BECKWITH
MARCO MASTROGIOVANNI
VIRGINIA GROSSO
RICHARD GROSSO
LAURIE KAY GROSSO
KATHARINE KING
DIANA DAVIDOW
DEBRAH CONSTANCE
CRAIG BEALER
JUDY BACA
DEBRA PADILLA
LAURA LAXINETA
MARILYN & IRVING LAXINETA
ROB WEISS
DALE NIELI
CAROL SCHLANGER
JEFFERY SCHWARTZ
DAVID WEISSMAN
MARC HUESTIS
PIERRE VUILLEUMIER
JUDY BRANFMAN
MICHELLE CAMERON
LOTHAR DELGADO

KAREN LANDRY
CHRIS MULKEY
LENORE REQUEIRA
WILLY MARQUEZ
JIM BALB
BOB SCHOMUS
SUSAN & RICHARD TITONE
JEAN FRAZBLAU
JENNIIFER LIM
MICHAEL KEARNS
MARY ANN CHERRY
JOHN FLECK
JUSTIN V BOND
GREG TRAVIS
DANIEL CAINER
JONATHAN CAINER
MARIE GORMAN
MARK GUGLIELMO
MARIO DI DONATO
SHELIA DI MARCO
CANDIDA ROYALLE
BETSY ZAJKO
JUDITH AVERY
PETER MC CARTHY
LARRY LITSKY
ANTONIO DIAS
ROBIN MEISEL
TONYA REED
JUDY GRAHAM
EDWARD VILGA
FELICE WILLAT
JESSICA COPEN
AMY FRIEDMAN
KAREN NEIBERG
S. SCOTT MAYERS
DARIEN MOREA

MAXINE NUNES
GRACE WESTON
LOTTI P KNOWLES
MAUREEN COTTER
ANNE MARIE SCHEFFLER
DAVID MILLER
DAVID WHEATLEY
DOM AVITABILE
SHAWN BARRY
CHRISTINA SCHLESINGER
KERRIE KILPATRIC-WEINBERG
LENNY LANZI
JOSEPH A LEVY
JANE CANTILLON
EVELYN DAITCHMAN
RANDALL CAPORALE
ESMARELDA KENT
DAVID EPSTEIN
BRIAN FRANK
JAN O'CONNOR
DENISE CANDIES
NICOLAS MELE
TITA FARRAR
MAUREEN TEEFY
DEBRA TRENT
SANDY MARTIN
GLENNA DUMEY
ALEX MEXI
CLAY BRAVO
ANINA LINCOLN
LULU
RAYNI
JOSHUA CHEON
BURLINGTON WILLES
M. CHILTON
CLAUDIA MILLER

CARMEL FRANCE
HELENA STANABACK
NATASHA YAR-ROUTH
BARRI ROUTH
LAURIE PROVOST
E BIANCHI
TIMOTHY CRAWFORD
JEFFERY GLENN
CHRISTOPHER BOHN
JAMES THOMAS
FUCHSIMWALDE

About the author:

Dolores De Luce has been a performer since 1970. She was mentored by the legendary Divine and the infamous gender-bending Cockettes. She has performed and written for many musical comedies and was nominated for 'Best Performer' by Bay Area Credits Association for Broken Dishes, a musical she co-wrote with Amber Waves.

Dolores' autobiographical screenplay, Grace Happens, based on this memoir was semi finalist at the Austin Screenwriting Competition. The Shirt, from *Gay Widow*, a collection of AIDS survivor stories, was published in Witness, an A.P.L.A. magazine.

Currently Dolores lives in Venice Beach and continues to write and act in TV commercials and film, while promoting her daughter Viva's singing career. She can be seen about town reading her stories with Queer Wise, an LGBTI senior writer's collective, and story-telling at The Moth, Tasty Words, Everybody Loves a Good Story, and other spoken word venues around Los Angeles. Contact www.counterculturediva.com

Photos by:
Dan Nicoletta is a San Francisco based freelance photographer who began his work in 1975 as an intern to Crawford Barton, staff photographer for *Advocate Magazine*. He worked in Harvey Milk's camera store in the heart of the burgeoning lesbian gay bisexual transgender Mecca in the Castro district and was also involved in Milk's victorious election to public office as one of the first openly gay elected officials in the world. Contact www.dannynicoletta.com

David Greene's collection of photographs called *Shameless* was exhibited in galleries in Berkeley, San Francisco, Chicago, New York, and Zurich. He also created photos for Gay Sunshine book, *Men Loving Men,* two of which are in the permanent collection of the Chicago Museum of Contemporary Art. David Greene's creative life has moved from film to photography to writing and his work includes two novels, *Unmentionables,* (2010) and *Detonate,* (2012). Contact www.DavidJGreene.com

Cover Design:
Jennifer Lim currently resides, works, surfs and plays in Venice Beach, California. Contact jenniferjadelim.com

www.ingramcontent.com/pod-product-compliance
Lightning Source LLC
Chambersburg PA
CBHW071409090426
42737CB00011B/1400